M000095752

FROM HARLEM TO HOLLYWOOD
MY LIFE IN MUSIC

FROM HARLEM TO HOLLYWOOD
MY LIFE IN MUSIC

BY

VAN ALEXANDER

WITH STEPHEN FRATALLONE

BearManor Media
2009

From Harlem to Hollywood
My Life in Music
© 2009 Van Alexander
with Stephen Fratallone

For information, address:

BearManor Media
P. O. Box 71426
Albany, GA   31708

bearmanormedia.com

Cover photo by Mitch Tobias

Cover design, typesetting and layout by John Teehan

Published in the USA by BearManor Media

ISBN—1-59393-451-3

TABLE OF CONTENTS

DEDICATION

For my dearest wife Beth, and to the rest of my beloved family, each and every one so very precious to me: Lynn, Joyce, Mitchell, JoAnne, Allison, Steve, Darren, Brooke, Andrew, Dorian, Bob and Brad. May you all set your goals in life and attain them.

– V.A.

2008

To Van Alexander, a big thank you for this opportunity and for your faith in me to forge ahead with this project and, above all, for your friendship. You are indeed not only a Great Gentleman of Music, but a Great Gentleman as well.

For Stephen and Rachel, with all my love.

– S. F.

2008

PREFACE

"You can have the men who make the laws, but give me the music makers."

— William Shakespeare (1564-1616)

There's an old joke that goes like this: "How do you get to Carnegie Hall?"

The answer: "Practice! Practice! Practice!"

Well, I got to Carnegie Hall not by practicing, but due to the talents of singer Michael Feinstein! That's the honest truth.

I wish that I could claim my own right musical artistry had landed me at one of the most prestigious and revered concert halls in the world, but I can't. My "15 minutes" of fame at Carnegie Hall came indirectly as a result of an arrangement I had written for a 47-year-old pop singer-musicologist who was making his concert debut there. I'm not knocking it by any means. I'll take whatever way I can to get into Carnegie Hall. Not every professional musician gets to perform there or has his or her music played there. Just being present on such "holy ground" was such a tremendous honor. And what a night it was! Wednesday, May 5, 2004, will always be etched in my mind and heart as a very special moment for me.

A few months earlier my good friend and former student, Johnny Mandel, was talking with Michael as he was gearing up for his debut at Carnegie Hall. Michael wanted to open his show by doing a twelve-minute medley of songs from the Big Band Era. Johnny told him that I would be the person to arrange that medley of tunes.

I had retired from music in 2003 and I thought I had left the "ring," if you will, undefeated. I was approaching my 89th birthday and figured it was time for me to relax a little. Then Michael called me and my "retirement" was short lived. I soon found that I was back in training.

Michael and I had a meeting about the music. He was uncertain as to what songs he wanted to use in the opening medley. I told him that the debut of jazz at Carnegie Hall came about with Benny Goodman's appearance there on January 16, 1938. Since this was going to be his debut at the esteemed concert hall, I suggested he do a medley of tunes associated with Benny. Michael loved the idea.

I went to work and put together a medley of songs for him and orchestrated it. The medley consisted of "Don't Be That Way," "Stompin' at the Savoy," "When Dreams Come True," "Goody Goody," "Gotta Be This or That," "What A Little Moonlight Can Do," and Benny's rousing flag-waver, "Sing, Sing, Sing."

Michael invited my wife Beth and me to come to New York to attend his Carnegie Hall performance. Our youngest daughter Joyce and her husband Harvey also made the trip to New York with us. I attended the rehearsal the afternoon of the performance and the 18-piece Big Band sounded super. Michael loved it!

I was pleasantly surprised when bandleader and composer Skitch Henderson came downstairs from his office at Carnegie Hall to listen to the rehearsal and to say hello. I had known Skitch for many years. In 1983 he founded the New York Pops Orchestra, which makes its home at Carnegie Hall. He served as the music director and conductor of the orchestra until his death the following year.

While growing up in New York there were numerous times when I passed the corner of 57th Street and Seventh Avenue, just two blocks south of Central Park, where Carnegie Hall is located. I was always impressed with this magnificent Italian Renaissance structure of narrow Roman bricks of a mellow ochre hue, with details in terracotta and brownstone, and I often thought of what the inside looked like. Carnegie Hall is one of the last large buildings in New York built entirely of masonry, without a steel frame. On a few occasions, I was able to sneak a few quick peeks inside the famous white-and-gold marble foyer, viewing with wide-eyed wonder its great slanting arches in the vaulted ceiling and the doors as well as the massive Corinthian columns in the corners embedded with intricate carvings.

It is understandable that this was steel magnate Andrew Carnegie's pride and joy when it first opened its doors in 1891. It was indeed a fabulous showplace for the rich and socially elite of New York society to hear some of the finest classical music performed. Now, 113 years and countless musical presentations later, I would have the rare opportunity of having some of my music performed at this bastion of fine arts and culture. Who would ever have thought of such a thing?

The night of Michael's performance, billed as *Michael Feinstein: The Great American Love Songs*, was filled with electricity and high emotional excitement. Carnegie Hall's main auditorium, now named after violinist Isaac Stern, seats 2,804 on five levels. The Main Hall is enormously tall, and visitors to the top balcony must climb 105 steps. All but the top level can be reached by elevator. Such an opulate ambieance was absolutely breathtaking!

A number of my relatives and friends also attended the sold-out concert. John Oddo, Michael's conductor, who previously was Rosemary Clooney's musical director for many years, led the Big Band in opening the show with Benny Goodman's theme song, "Let's Dance."

Michael performed the medley I had written magnificently and he received a thunderous ovation. When the applause and cheering subsided, Michael then introduced me to the audience, telling them that I had arranged the medley and how I was right there during the Swing Era by leading my own band and with my writing of "A-Tisket, A-Tasket" with Ella Fitzgerald. He had me stand up and take a bow amidst the audience's appreciative and exuberant applause. It was such a great night to savor and a night I would never forget.

As Michael's concert progressed, I couldn't help but think to myself how blessed and fortunate I've been not only in the 70 years in the music business, but also in life. I was born in Harlem, a place where some of the finest music of the era was created. I had the opportunity of arranging for Chick Webb's dynamite band, working with the fabulous Ella Fitzgerald and collaborating with her and Chick to produce a mega-hit recording of its day. I had a blast leading my own band for a time and having my arranging services clamored for by some of the top name bandleaders and singers of the day.

I was also fortunate in making the connections into radio, recordings, television and motion pictures when I moved out to Hollywood. I was honored to have worked so closely with singers Gordon MacRae and Dean Martin and a slew of other outstanding singers, actors, and musicians, and to receive three Emmy nominations and a Grammy Hall of Fame Award for "A-Tisket, A-Tasket."

While music has given me a wonderful life, nothing compares to the amazing life I have with my precious Beth. For the past 70 years, she's been my friend, lover, helpmate, confidant and most avid supporter of my work. Our daughters, Lynn and Joyce, are the apples of my eye, as are our grandkids and great-grandkids.

Yes, I've come a long way since those early days from Harlem and I've had a fabulous ride. But, now, at age 93, the "A" Train is not about to slow down quite yet. I'd like to share and reminisce with you a little as to how that ride went, if I may. All aboard!

                                        – Van Alexander
                                        Los Angeles, CA
                                        2008

FOREWORD

BY JOHNNY MANDEL

The first thing that comes to my mind whenever I think of Van Alexander is the word "swinging." He always wrote arrangements that swung. Maybe that's because he used to like to hang out at the Savoy Ballroom in Harlem and jitterbug. Look at all the swinging things he wrote for Chick Webb's orchestra. His arrangement of "A-Tisket, A-Tasket" for Chick's band made musical history. I always liked the way Van's band sounded and that was due to his writing.

I was fortunate to study under him for a few years and I got to learn from the best. That's how I got my start. Like most kids growing up at that time, I glued my ear to the radio listening to the sounds of the Big Bands. Every band in those days played the same song because the music publishers ran the music business. The biggest thing in the world for publishers was to get their songs played on the air. I was aware of songs, but I didn't know anything about the particulars of a song. I would hear one band over the radio and think to myself, "That was a pretty lousy song. I don't know what all the fuss was about." Then another band would come on the air and play the same song, and then I'd think, "How come I thought that was a lousy song? That sounds great!" Still another band would come on later and play the same song and I'd think, "That song was as bad as I thought it was." I was confused.

It wasn't long afterwards before the light went on in my head that I finally realized that the song itself had nothing to do with how it sounded. It was about whoever wrote the music for that song to be played that way. I wanted to know who did that sort of thing. I found out that person was called an arranger, and I knew then that's what I wanted to do.

I read an ad in *Down Beat* that Van Alexander was taking students to study arranging. I knew who Van Alexander was because they were playing a lot of his records on *Make Believe Ballroom* and other such radio shows. I pressured my mother in letting me study under Van, which she graciously did.

I convinced Van that I wanted to be an arranger. I learned more about arranging from his recording of "Stumbling" than I did from any other source. He introduced me to what is called a score. It's a snapshot of what everyone in the orchestra is doing for eight bars. The score he showed me was "Stumbling," a Zez Confrey song. It was a nice, bouncy tune. He then told me that now that I had seen what a score looked like, I now had to *hear* what it sounded like. While we were listening to this recording, Van showed me where we were at on the score, turning the pages as he went. He then said to me, "Now that you've seen what the piece looks like and have heard what it sounds like, all you have to do now is put these two things together in your head and you'll have it made." It sounded easy, but it wasn't.

He then gave me a big pad of yellow paper and told me to go home and write something and make sure that I find someone to play it. He said that the most important thing is to get people to play your music, no matter how good or bad it is, otherwise you'll never know what you wrote. In other words, he threw me in the water and yelled, "Swim!" There was no other way for me to start. I had to learn by doing.

Luckily for me, I was attending New York Military Academy on a band scholarship. I had enough guinea pigs in the school's jazz band to throw music at them to play. Van instilled in me the notion that if I got those two things together in my head, I would then be able to look at a score and get an idea of what it is going to sound like if it's played, or if I wanted to write something, I'd have to hear what it will look like; the reverse. It takes a long time to be able to do this, but that's how you do it. And he was right!

I started taking things off of records. I wanted to find out what made that sound sound like it did. I got hooked into that idea real early. I'd picture what that sound would look like on paper. I got to the point of recognizing the sounds of the band and being able to write down almost anything I heard. That was much of Van's doing as it was mine.

Van would also extend my musical education outside of his Manhattan apartment. He'd always invite me to his band rehearsals because he knew I was really into it. I got a great hands-on lesson because he showed me how everything I was learning came together.

He was loving and encouraging; the same guy he is now. I just happened to find the right mentor at the right time. Now at age 93, Van is still swinging. He continues to make beautiful music that is reflective of his beautiful soul. God love him!

– Johnny Mandel
Malibu, CA
2008

CHAPTER ONE

HARLEM NOCTURNE

The world was going to hell in a hand basket when I was born Alexander Van Vliet Feldman, on May 2, 1915. World War I, the "War to End All Wars," was raging in its ninth month around the globe. The Germans started using poison gas as a weapon of war while the British developed the tank as their own bludgeon of destruction. The Ottoman Empire began the systematic killings of its Armenian subjects, marking the beginning of the controversial Armenian Genocide. The British passenger liner, the *Lusitania*, was on the second day of its 202nd crossing of the Atlantic with 1,257 passengers, plus a crew of 702. Five days later, a German U-boat sunk the ship off the coast of Ireland killing 1,198 of the people aboard. Of that number, 128 Americans were lost out of 197, creating a U.S.-German diplomatic crisis for President Woodrow Wilson.

While isolationist America was keeping its eyes on world events, the Feldman Family was keeping their eyes on me. I was the second of two sons born to Jacob "Jack" Feldman and Mildred Van Vliet. My brother, David, was born three years ahead of me.

I came not into this world via a hospital bed but through the comfort of my mother's bed at 41 Convent Avenue near the corner of West 129th Street in what is commonly known in that section of Upper Manhattan as Harlem. Our apartment was just a few short blocks from City College of New York, St. Nicholas Park, and the famous Lewisohn Stadium, where my mother took me over the course of many summers as a youngster to hear wonderful outdoor symphony concerts that were performed there.

The entire block where we lived, bounded from 129th and 130th streets from St. Nicholas Terrace to Convent Avenue, contained seven standard six-story apartment houses that were built in 1910. The last time I visited New York I went to check out the old neighborhood as it has been several years since I had done so. It was then that I realized that the westernmost building, 41 Convent—named the St. Agnes—was a bit more unusual than the rest. It had bold Greek detailing and a sky-lit, barrel-vaulted lobby decorated in rich marble. The exterior was somewhat above the rather ordinary formula for such essentially middle-class structures.

While Harlem has long been associated with African-American culture, the tenants where we lived were white. It was during the Harlem Renaissance of the 1920s that central Harlem changed over to a predominately black tenancy. A few years ago, the New York City Landmarks Preservation Committee considered declaring the 41 Convent Avenue apartment building as a landmark site. I'd like to think that such a consideration had something in part to do with it being the place of my birth, but I'm not that vain. To my knowledge, a decision has yet to be reached by the Committee as to whether the building is worthy of landmark status. Maybe someday it will. The last I heard, the apartments—or co-op homes as they are called now—at 41 Convent Avenue were now selling between $81,000 and $96,000.

My father was born a Jew in Hungary, immigrating to the United States as an infant with his parents and four brothers in the late 1880s. He and his family were some of over 3,700,000 people who came to America from the Austrian-Hungarian Empire between 1820 and 1920. I never knew who his parents were. They died before I was born and Dad never talked much about his parents. However, he did talk about his brothers. They were spread out across the country so I didn't have any close connections with them while growing up. Later on, I did get to meet two of Dad's brothers. There was Uncle Al, who lived in Washington, D.C., and Uncle Henry, who I met when I came out to Los Angeles when I was working with Bob Crosby.

Dad was a pharmacist. He was a handsome man sporting dark hair. He stood about 5'11" tall and had a thin build to him physically, a trait which I inherited. Although Dad was born in Central Europe, he spoke without an accent and was American as apple pie. He was a very gentle, loving man.

My mother was born in an apartment on Cauldwell Avenue in the East Bronx in the late 1880s. She was a stunning blonde and always had a passion for music. She was a marvelous classical pianist. In the early days of radio, she had a non-paying 15-minute weekly sustaining program on WEAF, an NBC affiliate. That was due to her friendship with a famous radio announcer, Graham McNamee. Because my mother was a concert pianist, I was exposed to good music all the time. For that, I'm eternally grateful.

Mom also taught piano lessons privately. Throughout the week our apartment always seemed to buzz with excitement from her many piano students. One of Mom's students was Tommy Fulford, who was the piano man in Chick Webb's band when I worked with Chick. He took lessons from my mother in order to improve his playing technique.

When I turned six, my mother taught me how to play the piano and to read music. She made me practice daily. Like most young children that age, I didn't see the value of constantly practicing scales and arpeggios. In fact, I thought it pure drudgery. I would have preferred spending more time outside playing stickball in the street.

I often gave my mother a rough time about adhering to my practice schedule, thinking any way I could to avoid, or at the very least, forestall the inevitable. However, she was very firm but patient with me and because of my "stick-to-itiveness," eventually I came around to see the value of what she was trying to instill in me. Music for me then became fun, exciting, inspiring and challenging.

I was named after my maternal grandfather, Alexander Van Vliet, who was born in Rotterdam, Holland. That was reason enough for him to always drink to the Netherlands and toast to its then-reigning monarch, Queen Wilhelmina. Grandpa Alexander, who arrived in America as a young man in the early 1880s and who was proud of his Dutch heritage, would always quip, "If you ain't Dutch, you ain't much!"

My grandfather was a dashing-looking guy, bearing an uncanny resemblance to General John "Black Jack" Pershing. He and I had a close, loving relationship. He was always telling jokes. Some of that must have rubbed off on me as I find myself enjoying telling a good joke whenever I can.

Grandpa worked as the head keeper at the ominous Welfare Penitentiary on Welfare Island, the cigar-shaped, two-mile long island in the East River separating Manhattan and Queens. Previously known as Blackwell's Island, it become Welfare Island in 1921 and was renamed in 1973 as Roosevelt Island. The dismal-looking gray stone penitentiary stood 600 feet long and rose four stories high in a castle-like design and had 800 cells in four tiers back-to-back in the center of the structure. Entertainer Mae West once served time there. The place closed and was torn down in 1935 after the completion of a new penitentiary on Rikers Island, which now has the dubious distinction of being the world's largest penal colony.

My grandfather took me to visit Welfare Penitentiary once when I was about 10 years old. I knew Grandpa must have been a pretty tough guy because he carried a gun. Seeing the inmates and the tiers of cellblocks and hearing the repetitive loud clanging of cell doors didn't scare me in any way. I just thought the experience was "interesting."

It was while living in New York that my Grandpa Alexander met Bessie Coon, who hailed from London, England. She then became my maternal grandmother. Grandma Bessie never lost her English accent. Because of that she could never pronounce her "H's" well. It was very cute.

Having a mixture of Hungarian, Dutch, English and American in me, I guess I was sort of a League of Nations baby.

My father owned a Rexall drugstore just three short blocks north from our apartment, at the corner of West 131th Street and Amsterdam Avenue, right down the street from the old Knickerbocker Hospital. The Knickerbocker Hospital was founded in 1913 and it assumed the city's largest ambulance district for many decades and was a forerunner in treatments for polio, gynecology, and alcoholism.

Dad did quite well as a pharmacist and we lived very comfortably. I remember walking with my mother and brother many times to visit him at his store because he had a soda fountain, which made such visits all the more enjoyable. Chocolate ice cream floats were always on tap for David and me and we were always enthusiastically "ready, willing, and able" to dig in to such delectable delights at any given time!

I don't know how Mom and Dad met, but I'd like to think it had something to do with music. While they were married they certainly made beautiful music together. I grew up in a very loving, close-knit family. Mom and Dad were very good to their two boys. They sent my brother and me to experience summer camp in Vermont, which enabled us to get out of the hot and humid city for a few weeks. We also took frequent trips to Niagara Falls. The cool mist from those spectacular falls felt invigorating on my young face.

When I was about seven years old, Dad bought a lot and had a home built for us on Webb Avenue in the West Bronx. Although it was only six miles from the "old neighborhood," to my seven-year-old mind, it seemed like it was a million miles away. I attended nearby Public School No. 46 on 196th Street, which has now been renamed Edgar Allan Poe Elementary School. Upon completion of eighth grade, I graduated P. S. No. 46 in 1929.

I was a good kid while growing up and did the things kids usually do. I loved playing stickball with the other kids in the neighborhood, traded baseball cards, and cheered on the Yankees, our favorite baseball team. The Yankees' star centerfielder, Babe Ruth, was our hero and he literally helped to reinvent "America's Pastime" with his on-the-field prowess and his larger-than-life persona.

As all kids are prone to do, I also got into my share of mischief. One such incident that stands out very vividly in my mind and that scared the hell out of me occurred when I was about 13 years old. A school friend with whom I hung around suggested that we go down to 42nd Street to take in the sights. As we approached the subway station he gave me a "slug" nickel to use in the turnstile. I wondered why he gave me this phoney nickel to use so I asked him, "Why don't you use it?" He told me he also had one of his own. I knew it was wrong, but I put the slug nickel in the turnstile slot anyway. Sure enough, the subway attendant sitting on the other side knew I had used the bum coin to gain entrance onto the subway boarding ramp. He grabbed me by my jacket collar and detained me in the change booth while he went to retrieve the evidence. He then took me to the local police precinct.

The attendant called my father at 11 o'clock that evening and told him what I had done and that my bail was set at $500. My father told the man that he didn't have that kind of money at that time of night to get me out of jail. The attendant said I would then have to be kept at the precinct overnight.

Not knowing quite what to do, Dad then called Grandpa Alexander and told him what happened. In turn, my grandfather called the precinct to see how he could influence the situation. He told the desk sergeant who he was and he was assured that I would be well taken care of and that I would be released the following morning. I was.

The Interborough Rapid Transit Company (IRT), which ran the subway system in New York, was pretty aggressive in wanting to prosecute cases such as mine. My case then came up and I was extremely nervous. I wasn't sure what to expect. I went before the judge and he asked me, "Did you spend the night in jail?"

"Yes, sir," I replied.

"That should be punishment enough for you to never do this again," the judge replied as he dismissed my case with the pound of his gavel.

I let out an exhilerating and thankful sigh of relief. I learned my lesson well that day. I never got in that sort of trouble ever again.

We lived on Webb Avenue for six years, but eventually the distance between work and home became too much for Dad. He sold our Bronx home and we moved back to Upper Manhattan into a beautiful apartment overlooking Riverside Drive. It was here that I excitedly watched in awe as the George Washington Bridge was being built. What a sight that was to see! Construction began in 1927 and four years later the great suspension bridge opened, spanning the Hudson River, connecting New York with New Jersey. It is now one of the world's busiest bridges in terms of vehicular traffic.

Both my parents and grandparents were not particularly religious people. They believed in God, of course, but my brother and I never really grew up with any consistent formal religious training. David and I both went through our bar mitzvah ceremonies at age 13. That was about the only time we went to temple. As a family, we never really celebrated any of the major Jewish holidays like Passover or Hanukkah.

However, as far as any religious affiliation goes, my mother was a life-long student of Christian Science and the teachings of its founder, Mary Baker Eddy. A few of Mom's friends introduced her to it and it held her interest up until the day she passed away at age 86. I realize that on the surface it may seem contradictory to have one's mother as a student of Christian Science and one's father as a pharmacist living under the same roof, but in my case, it worked out well. My father was fine with anything my mother did. In fact, he was very receptive to my mother's interest in Christian Science. He'd tell her, "Whatever works for you, Dear, is OK with me."

A natural conflict exists between medicine and Christian Science. A true Scientist does not believe in medicine as a cure for one's ills, but rather, believes that one's mind and positive thinking will bring out needed healing. I learned that Christian Science is really a way of living; a proper way of thinking; a way of trying to constantly put mind over matter.

Dad's support for Mom's experience with Christian Science also saw him periodically attend worship services with her. Anytime my folks came to visit us in Los Angeles, they would attend Christian Science services on Rexford Drive in Beverly Hills. On occasion, they would take our two daughters, Lynn and Joyce, with them.

Mom tried to indoctrinate David and me with Christian Science teachings while we were growing up. I respectfully listened to her go on about it and I have to admit, I thought there were some good points to its principles, but I never embraced it fully. As I grew older, I couldn't see all its demands with the business I was in.

On the other hand, David, who later adopted our grandfather's surname as his own for professional reasons, fully embraced the teachings of Christian Science. He eventually became a Christian Science practioner and is still one to this day where he lives in Concord, Massachusetts. At age 97, he's listed in the *Christian Science Journal*. He helps people all over the world who believe in the principles of Christian Science.

Another interesting note about my remarkable brother, David…he designed the present-day flag of the United Nations. He sure did. After he was discharged from the Army at the end of World War II, David received a position at the United Nations as graphic designer. This was in 1946, at Lake Success, New York, before the United Nations moved to its present location in New York City. In the summer of 1947, he received the assignment to design the flag to include the official emblem of the United Nations with its polar projection in white of a world map centered on the North Pole enclosed in olive branches, a symbol of peace, against a sky-blue background. The flag was adapted by the United Nations Assembly on October 20, 1947, at Lake Success.

David has never been given the credit that is due to him for this project, nor does he solicit it. He's a very humble man who doesn't seek self-attention. That's just the kind of guy he is.

The only visible rift Mom had with Christian Science was when she became ill. She saw a doctor, so in practice she wasn't a true Scientist. But the teachings of Christian Science helped her in many areas of her life and it gave her the spiritual grounding she thought she needed.

When I was 14, Grandpa Alexander became ill with emphysema. His shortness of breath became so bad that my parents decided that it would best if Grandma Bessie and he would come to live with us. We needed to find a larger apartment in which to live and that meant moving once again. We didn't stay long at the Riverside Drive place. Needing a larger apartment that would house six people, we found a very spacious three-bedroom place at the six-story-high Southold Apartments on 150th Street and Broadway in the Washington Heights area of Upper Manhattan. It was here, I think, that I really started to grow up.

In the fall of 1929, I entered my freshman year at George Washington High School, located on Audubon Avenue in the Fort George neighborhood of Washington Heights, which bordered Harlem to the north.

Over the years, GWHS has distinguished itself with many noteable alumni. Some of my alma mater's more renowned success stories include actor and singer Harry Belafonte; international opera star Maria Callas (known then as Mary Anna Callas); Marvel and DC Comics artist Gene Colan; Alan Greenspan, economist and former Chairman of the Board of Governors of the Federal Reserve; Jacob Javits, the late U.S. Senator and former New York State Attorney General; Henry Kissinger, former U.S. Secretary of State and the 1973 winner of the Nobel Peace Prize; Major League Baseball Hall of Famer Rod Carew; Boston Red Sox slugger Manny Ramirez; actors Guy Williams (known then as Armando Joseph Catalano) and Ron Perlman; the late atomic scientist John George Kemeny; the late heavyweight boxer Bob Pastor (a.k.a. Robert E. Pasternak), and vocalist Helen Ward, who sang with Benny Goodman in the 1930s.

After school and on weekends, I helped care for my grandfather by shaving him and massaging his back whenever he felt tense. It was painful for me to see him deteriorate rather quickly right before my eyes.

Soon after I had turned 15, Grandpa Alexander died peacefully in bed. He was 71 years old. I felt I had lost a dear friend, which in many ways he was to me. I missed his warmth, his playfulness, and, of course, his jokes. Grandma Bessie continued to live with us. After my grandfather's death, I became more absorbed in music.

It was during the four years I spent at George Washington High School that my interest in music became more pronounced and focused, thus helping to shape my destiny.

CHAPTER TWO

STRIKE UP THE BAND

On a cool autumn day in early September 1929, I attended my first day at George Washington High School. The leaves on the trees were turning all sorts of different colors and there was briskness in the air. As a 14-year-old freshman I came to school a little anxious because I felt like I was a virtual stranger, not knowing very many of my fellow students. That feeling of anxiety soon passed as I got into my educational routine and I quickly made new friends.

In all honesty, I must admit that I was never a dedicated student. I passed all my grades, but my interest lay elsewhere—in music, music, music. The music bug had bitten me and I was infected. I wanted to participate in all music programs that GWHS had to offer. I joined the school marching band and since there are no parts written for piano in the marching band, I played the bass drum and cymbals. That was good experience as it allowed me to read drum and other percussion parts. I developed such a good rapport with the members of the band that after the first semester in marching band, I was promoted to drum major. It was great fun and I got to see all the football games for free.

One of the wonderful and endearing friendships that I was fortunate to have cultivated during my time at GWHS was with Henry "Butch" Stone. Butch was a standout alto saxophonist/novelty singer in my band and then went on to be a smash act with Jack Teagarden, Larry Clinton, and Les Brown. I first met Butch while we were members of the high-school marching band. He was a senior; I was a freshman. His warm and gregarious personality was evident even at that time and he was always full of quick wit and unpredictable but good-natured pranks. We "dug" each other from the first day we met.

Butch was an outstanding musician and was in demand playing with various local groups after graduating high school in 1930. For the past 80 years, Butch and I have remained close friends. He retired recently as a featured performer with the Les Brown Band of Renown. Butch and his lovely wife, Shirley, live 12 short miles away in Van Nuys, California, and he and I talk on the phone to each other almost daily.

Things were going well for me that first semester in school until Tuesday, October 29, came around. That day has been known as "Black Tuesday," the day the stock market crashed ushering in for the next decade the Great Depression. It would be the longest and most severe depression ever experienced by the industrialized Western world.

Being a teenager, I wasn't really cognizant of what all that meant. We were in our own worlds. I remember overhearing our teachers talking about it with great concern, and I heard of people jumping off buildings to their deaths because of financial ruin, but I never personally witnessed anything that drastic ever happening.

This wasn't a time of financial disaster for our family. Dad lost some money in holdings he had on second mortgages, but that was the extent of his financial losses. It didn't break us. There was always a need for a pharmacist in the community, so our family was never in dire economic straits. However, witnessing soup kitchens spring up all around town and men standing in line, sometimes at blocks length in order to get a hand out, were rather disturbing sights.

It was during my high-school years that I glued myself in front of the family radio whenever I could, listening to the various bands and vocal groups that were doing broadcast remotes. I also loved the vocal styling of the Mills Brothers and how they imitated instruments with their voices. I also listened to a lot of recordings of popular bands such as Paul Whiteman, Benny Goodman, the Casa Loma Band with Glen Gray, and, of course, Louis Armstrong. I never dreamed that I'd be writing arrangements for them someday.

As a result of the excitement I derived from music, I became fascinated with the mechanics of how a song was orchestrated. I took special interest in how the sounds of each instrument in an ensemble were systematically utilized to weave a vibrant musical tapestry that was not only pleasing to the human ear, but which also told a story. Such an aural tapestry is commonly known as an arrangement. As I listened more closely to the music, I began to realize that it's the arrangement that makes a song sound either like a million bucks or ten cents. As I've always said, "An arranger is a songwriter's best friend."

I had no formal training in orchestration and arranging at this juncture of my young musical journey. There weren't any "how-to" books available on the subject. My early education involved lots of trial-and-error. I began to experiment with orchestration by putting together a small eight-piece dance band. The ensemble consisted of piano, drums, string bass, a trumpet, a trombone, and three saxophones. I, of course, played piano. My two good friends, Sid Segan and Artie Stein, played drums and alto saxophone, respectively. The other members (whose names I don't remember) were just music-minded guys who jumped at a chance to just rehearse.

I don't recall the name of that first piece of music I had arranged; however, I do remember when my band played it, it sounded pretty good. I was hooked and I knew that this was what I wanted to do in life.

Throughout high school I continued to play in the school marching band, symphony orchestra, and pep band while still privately experimenting with music and arranging. The arrangements were getting better, although they still sounded rather primitive to my ear.

My first gig as a bandleader, if you will, came when I was a freshman. My same eight-piece band entered the Battle of the Bands contest at William Fox's Audubon Theater on 165th Street and Broadway. What a beautiful place it was!

The 2,368-seat theater, which opened in 1912, and was noted for its vaudeville acts and movies, also had a ballroom upstairs on the second floor that was used for social occasions and special events. The facade of the theater facing Broadway included a three-dimensional polychrome terra-cotta design of a boat (representing the Argo of Jason and the Argonauts) with the face of Neptune on it, two faces of court jesters, and icons in the form of fox heads to represent the owner of the building, William Fox. Within the theater were box seats adorned with fabric curtains and Bentwood chairs that were in the art-nouveau style. A satyr's head crowned each box that had been flanked by maidens with diaphanous dresses.

In 1965, the Audubon Theater was also the place of the assassination Black Muslim leader Malcolm X. Shortly after that violent act occurred, the Audubon closed its doors. It is now home to the Harlem-Heights Historical Society and to the Malcolm X Museum.

I led a Guy Lombardo-type band, called Sid Allan and His Orchestra. I took my drummer friend's first name, Sid Segan, and used a derivative of my first name, Allan, as my last name. I thus became Sid Allan. To give our merry group a more professional look, our parents helped to subsidize a large sign emblazoned with gold lettering that read, "Sid Allan and His Orchestra." It was prominently placed behind the band wherever we played.

My worthy challenger on this night of competition was another teen bandleader, Lee Kuhn. His band sounded like Freddy Martin's with a tenor saxophone lead. Playing saxophone in Lee's band was my friend, Butch Stone.

We played the opening set and received a hardy round of applause for our efforts. Then Lee Kuhn and his group played their set, fairing about as well as we did, until Butch was introduced, who came out from the sax section to do a comedy routine that broke the place up.

The winner of this coveted event was decided by audience applause. It was a prehistoric version, if you will, to what *American Idol* is today on television. After both bands played, Lee and I stood together on stage for the final decision. The theater's master of ceremonies, Fred Lowry, who promoted the event, put his hand over my head, which solicited robust audience applause. Next, he placed his hand over Lee's head and the reaction was about the same. Then Butch came out from behind the curtain and the applause and cheers became deafening. Lee and his boys won hands down, taking home the $25 cash prize and silver trophy.

Even though Sid Allan and His Orchestra lost the Battle of the Bands, they continued to play at various local gigs, including dances held in school gymnasiums and at the YMCA.

During my senior year I assembled a seven-piece band made up of fellow student musicians in the hopes of playing for the senior prom. I contacted Luther Gloss, the head of the high-school music department, and he suggested that I talk about it with the Senior Prom Committee.

I approached the five-member Senior Prom Committee and gave them my pitch as to why my band should be the one to play for the prom. The Committee wanted to hold an audition so they could hear what the band sounded like. I told my mother about it and she suggested that the audition be held in the living room of our Southold Apartment because none of us drove and we had no other place to rehearse or audition. I relayed that suggestion to the Committee and they agreed to come to my place to hear us.

On the afternoon of the audition, Mom and I frantically cleared out the furniture in our living room. The guys in the band came early to set up. The band consisted of three saxes, one trumpet, drums, bass, and me at the piano (it was Mother's Steinway concert grand). The members of Senior Prom Committee also brought ten seniors along to get their opinions as to how we sounded. I was flabbergasted! We had a good-size living room but even at that, 23 people crowded together in a confined area made for a pretty tight squeeze!

We played a few stock arrangements and a few special pieces I had arranged and we got the job! It was a non-paying job, but it was huge feather in our caps to know that we were good enough to play for the senior prom. The prom itself wasn't until the end of the semester so I had time to write a few more arrangements that we thoroughly rehearsed.

Our senior prom was very tame in comparison to high-school proms of today. Dress for the affair was casual. Guys did not wear tuxedos, nor did girls wear formal dresses. There were no corsages, no limousines. Couples danced close together, not apart from each other. Our band played a fine mixture of slow and fast numbers while the kids danced the popular dance steps of the day such as The Shag, The Charleston, and The Lindy Hop.

Although music was my main focus while in high school, I also got focused on girls. I had quite a few girlfriends while in high school. A few names that come to mind are Christine Pixley, Margie Lawless, Doris Eisenberg, and Frieda Amchin, who was voted the prettiest girl in the senior class (more about her later). There was also Gladys Krupp. My mother couldn't stand her. Finally, there was a girl named Beth Baremore. My mother loved her!

I first met Beth at The Point, a local ice cream parlor just down the street from George Washington High School. It was a popular place where kids hung out after school. I was a sophomore and she was a freshman. There was a mutual attraction between us. To me, she was a knockout with her 5'2" frame, dark hair, infectious smile and gregarious personality. She also had a great pair of legs, or "gams," as we called them back in those days.

In June 1933, I graduated from high school. I kept busy during this time as a working musician. I joined Local 802 of the Musicians' Union. Through the union, the Sid Allan Orchestra got booked for a three-week gig at The Jockey Club in Washington, D. C. In addition, we played for a number of fraternity parties and we were regulars at the Club Fordham in the Bronx playing for Saturday night dances.

I was also constantly studying and analyzing symphonic scores and other musical charts to further my self-study in music and in orchestration.

Finding the need to acquire some formal education in music, I enrolled in nearby Columbia University to take some extension courses in music. While the courses themselves were interesting, I didn't get much out of them as they primarily focused on classical music. I was too eager to get some formal training in arranging for swing bands.

At the same time I began studying orchestration and composition with Otto Cesana, a fine composer and teacher. Pianist Ray Barr, also a GWHS alumnus and who later played in my band and who worked for many years with singer Frankie Laine, recommended him to me. Señor Cesana was noted for his famous composition. "Symphony in Jazz," and in later years, was labeled as a forerunner in the "easy listening" music category. His studio was in Aeolian Hall, a concert hall near Times Square in Midtown Manhattan. This is where I was first truly exposed to the full orchestra—strings, woodwinds, brass and percussion.

Señor Cesana was a thorough musician and teacher. He was low-key but diligent and very patient. I studied with him for a year and he was pleased and impressed as to how quickly I learned my lessons. He was always very enthusiastic and encouraging about the various musical scores I was working on.

During the summers of 1934-1936, my seven-piece band, now known as Al Feldman and his Orchestra, was booked into some of the better hotels in the Catskill Mountains, less than 100 miles from home. The Catskills are a traditional vacation land with many summer resorts and camp grounds. It's famous for being the site of the so-called "Borscht Belt," a collection of Jewish resorts (Brown's, Grossinger's, etc.) where many young Jewish stand-up comics and entertainers got their start.

Members of my band included Artie Stein, alto saxophone and clarinet; Dan Forrest and Joe Rossetti, violins; Larry Jacobs, trumpet; Hal Worth, trombone; and Carl Kent, drums. We worked as waiters/musicians at the President Hotel in Swan Lake, the Livingston Manor in White Roe Lake, and the Flager in Ellenville. God, we had fun! I got to meet and accompany many future stars such as Danny Kaye, Jackie Miles, and singer Jan Peerce. The food at these resort areas was great and the fringe benefits were terrific… especially the girls!

The experience I gained as a bandleader playing in the Catskills was invaluable. It set the stage for me to go on to the next level of my career, which involved a daring encounter that turned into a wonderful associa-tion with a small, black, hunchback drummer who led one of the most exciting and explosive bands to ever come out of Harlem.

Left: Here I am at age 2. This was the last time I ever rode a horse.

Right: At age 6, I was ready to command the troops to victory!

Left: My parents
Jacob Feldman
and Mildred
Van Vliet in
1950.

Right: My father Jacob
Feldman in 1940.

Above: The Four Feldman Brothers:
(L to R) Jacob, Al, Charles, and Henry.

Left: My brother David Van Vliet in
France in 1945.

Above: My maternal grandparents Alexander Van Vliet and Bessie Coon. Grandpa Alexander came from Holland and Grandma Bessie emigrated from England. I was very close to both of them.

Left: My grandfather Alexander Van Vliet dressed in his prison guard's uniform. He is the spitting image of General John "Black Jack" Pershing.

Right: The ominous-looking Welfare Island Penitentiary where my Grandpa Alexander worked as a prison guard. The cigar-shaped two-mile long island is located in the East River separating Manhattan and Queens. The prison is no longer there. It was renamed Roosevelt Island in 1973 and is now a residential community.

Left: The flag of the United Nations that my brother David Van Vliet designed in 1947.

Left: Me looking dashing at age 21.

Above: My early band—The Al Feldman Orchestra – The Catskills – 1934.
Front Row (L to R): Al Feldman, piano/leader; Dan Forest, violin;
Joe Rossetti, violin; and Artie Stein, alto saxophone/clarinet.
Back Row (L to R): Carl Kent, drums; Larry Jacobs, trumpet;
and Hal Worth, trombone.

CHAPTER THREE

STOMPIN' AT THE SAVOY

A lot of us teenagers and young adults all loved to dance. And *the* place to dance was the Savoy Ballroom, located on Lenox Avenue between 140th and 141st Streets, right in the heart of Harlem.

Owned by Moe Gale (Moses Galewski), a Jewish businessman, and managed by Charles Buchanan, a black Harlem real-estate businessman, the Savoy Ballroom opened its doors on March 12, 1926. The Savoy was one of the first racially-integrated public places in the country, and for 32 years was billed as the "World's Finest Ballroom." It occupied the second floor of a building that extended along the whole block between 140th and 141st Streets, and featured a large dance floor (200 feet by 50 feet), two bandstands, and a retractable stage. The ground floor of the building housed the entrance to the ballroom at the center of the block signified by the marquee that extended out over the sidewalk and various stores. The Savoy was appropriately nicknamed, "The Home of Happy Feet," and it was also known among the regular patrons as "The Track" for the elongated shape of the dance floor. Many of the jazz dance crazes of the 1920s and 1930s originated there such as The Lindy Hop and The Big Apple. The Savoy closed its doors for good on July 10, 1958, and was torn down. A housing complex called the Delano Village took its place. A plaque near the site now marks with nostalgic reverie the cultural impact this famed dance spot had not only on Harlem itself, but on America as well.

The main reason why the Savoy swiftly became the most popular dance venue in Harlem was largely due to the marvelous black bands that played there. They played fabulous arrangements and had exciting musicians. Even though I went there to dance, I also was always listening critically to the great arrangements of these bands. I was studying orchestration and arranging with Otto Cesana at the time and I was trying to

21

"hear" what he was teaching me in relation to what was going on musically with these bands.

Some of the bands that frequented the Savoy that I really "dug" were those of dynamic front man and showman Lucius Venable "Lucky" Millinder; saxophonist Don Redman, who, incidentally, was a brilliant arranger in his own right; vocalist Willie Bryant, who became best known in the 1950s as the regular emcee at the Apollo Theater; trumpeter Erskine Hawkins, known as the "Twentieth Century Gabriel," who also composed the Big Band Era standard, "Tuxedo Junction"; and saxophonist Teddy Hill, who later went on to manage Minton's Playhouse in Harlem, the birthplace of bebop jazz. In 1937, Hill had a young kid playing third trumpet in the band by the name of John Birks Gillespie, who later became known as the great "Dizzy" Gillespie, one of the early icons of bebop.

While all the aforementioned bands thrilled me, none thrilled me more than the one led by that outstanding diminutive hunchback drummer, Chick Webb. He was my favorite. In 1931, his band became the house band at the Savoy. His band consistently packed musical punch with its hard-driving swinging arrangements which, in turn, always rocked the house. Propelling that drive was the band's sparkplug, little Chick himself.

William Henry "Chick" Webb was born on February 10, 1909, in Baltimore, MD. Early in his life, Chick had been accidentally dropped on his back, smashing several vertebrae. As a result, he fought off congenital tuberculosis of the spine that left him hunchbacked. He never fully grew, becoming dwarf-like with a large face and broad shoulders. Playing drums helped to strengthen his body. Even though he was small in stature—standing less than five feet tall—and hunchback, he was a genius and the people loved him. Chick may have been a small man, but he was sure big to those of us who loved his music.

Chick was universally admired by drummers for his forceful sense of swing, accurate technique, control of dynamics, and imaginative breaks and fills. He became one of the best-regarded bandleaders and drummers of the new "Swing" style. Drumming legend Buddy Rich cited Webb's powerful technique and virtuoso performances as heavily influential on his own drumming, and even referred to Webb as "the daddy of them all."

Unlike earlier drummers, Chick used the woodblocks and cowbell only for momentary effects, and varied his playing with rim shots, temple-block work, and cymbal crashes. In his celebrated two-to-four-bar fills, he abandoned earlier jazz drumming formulae for varied mixtures of double-

and triple-meter patterns. Chick used custom-made pedals, gooseneck cymbal holders, a 28-inch bass drum and a wide variety of other percussion instruments to create thundering solos of complexity and energy. He was seldom given to long solos, but when he did solo, he was tasteful, exciting and flawless. He played perched high upon a platform in the center of the ensemble. He was quite a sight to behold! He looked like a reigning monarch surveying his kingdom—his "Kingdom of Swing," if you will, and rightly so. After all, Chick was hailed as "The King of the Drums."

In 1934, Chick recorded a handful of Edgar Sampson tunes that did well for him commercially: "If Dreams Come True" (January 15), "Stompin' at the Savoy," named in honor the famous dance spot (May 18), and "Blue Lou" (November 19). The following year Ella Fitzgerald joined the band as the "girl singer." When Ella came on board, Chick's stock portfolio increased.

After many visits to the Savoy, I had developed what I called a "nodding acquaintance" with Chick. He'd shake his head and say, "Hi, kid." And I'd reply, "Hi, Chick," in return.

One cold snowy night in early February 1936, I got enough nerve to approach Chick after he had played the last set of the evening and said, "Chick, I've got a couple of arrangements at home that might fit your band, if you're interested. Would you like to hear them?"

"Sure, bring them to rehearsal next Friday," he replied.

Well, I was bluffing. I didn't have any such arrangements. I was, however, thrilled and excited that Chick even considered my offer. This would be my first opportunity to arrange for a full-size dance band: three trumpets, two trombones, four saxophones, and four rhythm (piano, bass, guitar, and drums). I went home that night and for the next three days and nights I wrote out those two arrangements: the Dixieland classic, "That's a Plenty," and "Keepin' Out of Mischief Now," a Fats Waller and Andy Razaf composition.

I was very familiar with the band's style so it didn't take me that long to come up with a finished product. I completed both arrangements by Tuesday of the following week. I was very excited. I couldn't wait until Friday rolled around. When that day finally came, I arrived at The Savoy early. However, unbeknownst to me, Chick conducted his band rehearsals *after* the job. The last dance set ended at 1 a.m. The guys would then have about an hour break to have something to eat and maybe down a few glasses of Muscatel wine. The rehearsal actually didn't start until around 2 a.m.

Chick had some excellent arrangers in his band who were also his regular musicians, guys like saxophonists Edgar Sampson and Wayman Carver. Although not a regular band member, Charlie Dickson wrote some great arrangements for the band as well.

Edgar had a few new tunes he brought to the rehearsal, so his pieces were played first. Edgar had been with Chick's band from almost the beginning. He was a great contributor to the band's library and all the guys in the band loved him. He was really the *true* writer of "Stompin' at the Savoy," although Benny Goodman and Chick were named as *de facto* co-collaborators on the tune. Edgar penned other notable tunes such as "Don't Be That Way" and "Lullaby in Rhythm." He left Chick's band in mid-1936 with a reputation as a composer and arranger that led to freelance work with Goodman, Artie Shaw, Red Norvo, and Teddy Wilson, among others. He continued to play sax through the late 1940s and started his own band (1949-1951). He was nicknamed "The Lamb" because he was so mild-mannered and gentle. He was a gentleman of the old school. Edgar and I corresponded many years later, before he passed away in 1973, at age 70. He and I were pretty close friends.

After Edgar's pieces were played, Chick and the band then rehearsed some things that were written by Wayman and Charlie Dickson (who died in December 1940 at age 42). Wayman was one of the earliest and one of the few jazz flautists active in the swing era. In 1934, he joined Chick's band playing both saxophone and flute, after having previously worked and recorded with Elmer Snowden and Benny Carter, among others. While with Chick, Wayman wrote several arrangements, of which "Spinning the Web" was among the most notable. Others are "Down Home Rag," "Tain't What You Do," "My Heart Belongs to Daddy," and "Holiday in Harlem." He also wrote, arranged and copyrighted an original, "Swinging on the Reservation," that featured Ella Fitzgerald on the vocal that was recorded in the fall of 1936. Wayman was well-featured on four 1937 titles by Chick Webb and his Little Chicks, a quintet matching his flute with Chauncey Haughton's clarinet, who joined the band late that summer. These small group recordings were examples of early jazz chamber music at its best. Wayman remained with the orchestra for a few months, as it continued under Ella's leadership after Chick's death (1939), and he eventually settled in Atlanta as a professor of music at Clark College. He died in 1967 in Atlanta, at age 61.

By the time the guys in the band got to my arrangements, it was close to 5 a.m. They were a little tired but they played my tunes with all the verve and gusto that had become their trademark.

What a thrill it was for me to hear Chick Webb and his dynamite band play *my* arrangements! To me, every guy in the band was an all-star—the "Murderer's Row," if you will, of swing. There was Mario Bauza, Bobby Stark and Taft Jordan in the trumpet section; and Sandy Williams and Nat Story on trombones. Chick nicknamed his brass section "The Five Horseman." On saxophones were Pete Clark, Edgar Sampson, Teddy McRae and Wayman Carver. Rounding out this stellar group was Tommy Fulford on piano; John Trueheart on guitar; and Beverly Peer on string bass, who later played with cabaret pianist/singer Bobby Short.

Chick and the guys loved my scores and Chick paid me $20 on the spot for the two arrangements. He didn't have the money on him at the moment, so he took an advance from Charlie Buchanan, the manager of the Savoy. It was my first sale and, for this 20-year-old budding arranger, I was ecstatic beyond description. I went home on Cloud Nine...and Ten!

My excitement and celebratory mood was abruptly curtailed, though, when I returned home just as the sun was rising. Since I hadn't come home by my usual time (around 2 a.m.), my mother was in a panic. Just about the time Chick and the guys were playing my tunes, she called the police frantically telling them "My son is in Harlem. My God, what can he be doing there so late? I hope that he is all right!"

A short time after her prodigal son explained what had happened, all was forgiven. Mother and son relationship was once again restored. Once their blood pressures came back down to normal, both my parents were then elated at the news of my good fortune.

Chick then hired me to write three arrangements a week for the band at a whopping salary of $75 per week, which included me having to hand-copy each and every band part. That was pretty good money in those days, certainly more than I had ever earned. Plus, I was doing what I wanted to do while working for my favorite band. Life couldn't get any better.

I guess my salary was indeed pretty good since all I had to write out were thirteen band parts and not fourteen. I didn't have to write out any drum parts because Chick didn't read music at all. All he had to do was hear an arrangement once, and he memorized it, and through his own ingenious ear, he amplified what I would write. In fact, I don't remember ever writing a drum part for him.

Chick liked my arrangement of "Keepin' Out of Mischief Now" so much that the following week the band made a transcription recording of it along with a batch of other tunes. While transcription recordings were made for radio play only, I was overjoyed to no end that the piece was documented on wax. I had to pinch myself to make sure that I wasn't dreaming!

Although I wrote some early instrumental pieces for the band, Chick wanted me to concentrate on writing things for his up-and-coming female band vocalist, Ella Fitzgerald.

Ella Jane Fitzgerald was born on April 25, 1917, in Newport News, Virginia. She moved to New York as a child, experiencing a difficult family life. In November 1934, the then-17-year-old Ella won an amateur singing contest held at the Apollo Theater. In January 1935, she won the chance to perform for a week with the Tiny Bradshaw band at the Harlem Opera House. It was there that she first met Chick, who was looking for a female vocalist to help boost public interest in the band. He had already hired Charlie Linton, a handsome singer, to work with the band. Chick had some initial misgivings about Ella because she was not glamourous looking as other "canaries," a nickname girl singers were called then. "She was gawky and unkempt, a diamond in the rough," he was later quoted as saying. He offered her the opportunity to test with his band when they played a dance at Yale University. Despite the rough crowd, Ella was a great success, and from then on, she was a member of the band.

Ella easily won over the Savoy Ballroom crowd (including this young fan!) and Chick soon realized he had a valuable asset in Ella. She cut her first sides with the band on June 12, 1935, with "I'll Chase the Blues Away" (released on the Brunswick label, a subsidiary of Decca Records) and "Love and Kisses." The latter tune, released on Decca, was a commerical dance band arrangement aimed at reaching a broad audience. And it worked.

Ella quickly caught on with the public, so Chick featured her more and more. He saw in her a commercial future for his music. The band itself, which had developed as a powerful musical entity of its own, began playing a smaller role, and its sound and character were changing. Chick was commercializing his band to target "white" America, where the money lay.

Ella was so popular and presented such commercial appeal that Chick used her on nearly every one of his recording sessions. There were exceptions, of course. Charles Linton was featured on a couple of songs: "Are You Here to Stay?" (June 12, 1935) and "Moonlight and Magnolias" (October 12, 1935). Trumpeter Taft Jordan was given "I May Be Wrong"

(October 12, 1935) and he later recorded a duet with Ella on my arrangement of the tune "Ella" (June 9, 1938). After saxophonist Louie Jordan joined the band during the summer of 1936, he did the vocals on my arrangements of "Gee, But You're Swell" (January 15, 1937), "Rusty Hinge" and "Wake Up and Live" (both on March 24, 1937) and "There's Frost on the Moon" (January 15, 1937). The latter two pieces were built around a vocal trio consisting of Ella, Charles, and Louie.

During this period Chick recorded only a handful of those exciting swinging instrumentals for which his band was noted: "Clap Hands! Here Comes Charley!" and "That Naughty Waltz" (both on March 24, 1937); "Strictly Jive" (October 27, 1937); "Squeeze Me" and "Harlem Congo" (November 1, 1937); "Midnite in a Madhouse (Midnite in Harlem)" (December 17, 1937); "Spinnin' the Web" (May 3, 1938); and "Who Ya Hunchin'?" (August 18, 1938).

I was fortunate to have contributed two big instrumental arrangements to Chick's library: "Azure" (May 2, 1938) and "Liza," recorded the following day. I wrote a slow and moody take on Duke Ellington's "Azure." I was really proud of that arrangement. It's a pretty piece. At the time I wrote it, Chick had secured a sustaining radio program on WJZ (the Blue Network) in New York, with a new black vocal group called the Ink Spots. "Azure" was going to be featured on the show. I was so excited that I called my parents, other relatives and friends to have them tune in to the broadcast. At the last moment, the producer of the show pulled the song from the broadcast thinking it would slow down the pace of the show too much. I was crestfallen, but there wasn't much I could do about it.

The other tune, "Liza," showcased Chick on drums. It's about the only recording where he is prominently featured on drums. A number of publications at the time—and even today—mistakenly gave credit for the arrangement to Benny Carter. Benny, who played in Chick's band in 1931, and who went to be a highly respected bandleader, composer and arranger, had said publicly many times that it was my arrangement.

When I first met Ella, she was a shy young lady and very humble. I initially thought that she might be a bit cocky and into herself, but she wasn't that way at all. She had a gentle way about her, yet she was loaded with bridled enthusiasm as only a teenager could have. That enthusiasm came across loud and clear in her singing. She had an infallible ear. Her intonation was impeccable and her phrasing just marvelous. As time went on, Ella gained more self-confidence and her singing became more polished, more mature.

The first recorded piece that I had arranged for Ella was a John Henry Hopkins Jr., and J.C. Johnson tune about love that had gone awry called "Crying My Heart Out For You." It was waxed for Decca on April 7, 1936.

Less than two months later—on June 2—Chick and crew were back in the Decca recording studio cutting five sides, all featuring Ella. One of those sides that I had arranged—a bouncy Hoagy Carmichael ditty called "Sing Me a Swing Song (And Let Me Dance)"—would turn out to be her first hit single. The tune reached number eighteen on the charts for one week in July.

With the success of "Sing Me a Swing Song," Ella came more into her own and was not looked upon anymore as just "Chick Webb's band singer." She even caught the attention of Benny Goodman, who somehow got her to record three tunes with his band for Victor Records on November 5 in the absence of Helen Ward, his regular band vocalist. Ella was under contract to Decca, and so this recording session caused all kinds of legal complications. The most popular cut from that tritium and the one that had somehow survived the litigation battles was "Goodnight, My Love."

Ella's second hit with Chick, "You'll Have to Swing It," her ode to "Mr. Paganini," recorded on October 29, peaked at number twenty for a week in December.

To be honest, the material that Ella was singing had no substance. In fact, a lot of it was pure junk. Even Ella was concerned about the material she was asked to perform. She wanted to make a hit record and she felt that the songs she was asked to sing wouldn't help her to accomplish that goal. Most of her stuff was "bubble gum" music that dealt with such teenage ideologies as dancing, swing music, or how swing music affected her. She would also name-drop Chick Webb's name somewhere in the lyrics, too—another good commercial ploy. But what she recorded seemed to grab listeners' ears. That's what Chick wanted, so it worked.

Other arrangements I did for Ella that were recorded include "Devoting My Time to You" (June 2, 1936); "Vote For Mr. Rhythm" and "I've Got the Spring Fever Blues (both on October 29, 1936); "Take Another Guess" (January 14, 1937); "Wake Up and Live," "It's Swell of You," "You Showed Me the Way," "Cryin' Mood," and "Love is the Thing, So They Say" (all on March 24, 1937); "Just a Simple Melody" (October 27, 1937); "I Want To Be Happy" (November 2, 1937); "The Dipsy Doodle" and "Hallelujah!" (both on December 17, 1937); "Pack Up Your Sins and Go to the Devil," "McPherson is Rehearsin' (To Swing)," "Everybody Step" (all June 9, 1938); "Wacky Dust, "Gotta a Pebble in My Shoe" (a collaborative piece written by lyricist Charlie Tobias and me), and "I Can't Stop Lovin' You" (all on August 17, 1938); "F.D.R. Jones," "I Love Each Move You Make" and "I Found My Yellow Basket," the follow-up tune to "A-Tisket, A-Tasket" (all on October 6, 1938).

Ella also recorded a number of small group sides for Decca under her own name called "Ella Fitzgerald and Her Savoy Eight." Members of the Savoy Eight included Chick and key members of his band: trumpeter Taft Jordan, trombonist Sandy Williams, clarinetist Pete Clark, tenor saxophonist Teddy McRae, pianist Tommy Fulford, guitarist John Trueheart, and bassist Beverly Peer. Later variations of this group also included Louie Jordan and Hilton Jefferson on alto saxophones and Bobby Johnson on guitar. I wrote a couple of arrangements for this small group: "Organ Grinder's Swing" and "My Last Affair" (both on November 18, 1936), and "I Was Doing All Right" (January 25, 1938). Ella seemed to be more relaxed and freer in this musical setting than with the Big Band. Her jazz sensibility on these small group recordings was astounding.

The year 1937 proved to be a big year for Chick, Ella and the band. Chick was now gaining lots of attention due to radio broadcasts. Radio exposure was highly sought after by bands as a way of getting recognized with the public and in turn, making it big. Chick had eight radio slots a week, more than any other band at the time. He was having Ella cover many of the pop tunes of the day, succumbing to the pressures of the song pluggers who wanted to get their songs onto the charts, which were based on the number of times a song was played on the air during a seven-day week. Such a move paid off. Ella chalked up still another hit—my arrangement of "Rock it For Me," recorded November 1, 1937—which went to number nineteen on the Hit Parade chart early the following year. In the meantime, Ella was voted Number One Female Vocalist in the first-ever *Down Beat* and *Melody Maker* readers' polls, ahead of rivals Billie Holiday and Mildred Bailey.

Chick Webb and Ella Fitzgerald were becoming synonymous with each other. Gigs were no longer being promoted as "Chick Webb and his Orchestra," but as "Chick Webb and his Orchestra featuring Ella Fitzgerald," or just simply "Chick and Ella."

This was the year that also saw Chick being invited to participate in a number of extra-musical activities. One such event was the brainchild of Milt Gabler, who owned the nine-foot-wide Commodore Music Shop on East 42nd Street, and jazz philanthropist John Hammond. Both men wanted to promote small group jazz while helping to boost record sales.

Gabler loved the spontaneous small group jazz format. They persuaded a host of notable musicians into playing free for Gabler's customers at Sunday afternoon jam sessions. Benny Goodman and Gene Krupa volunteered their services; so did Duke Ellington, Artie Shaw, and Chick, and members of the Count Basie band. Gabler rented empty recording studios for his sessions and they proved successful.

On one particular Sunday, Duke Ellington, Artie Shaw and Chick teamed up for rousing jam session at the Brunswick recording studio. Yours truly was there as was jazz journalist and producer Helen Oakley Dance. A photo of the session was taken and includes me peering from behind the crowd sporting an enthusiastic grin on my face. The photo is now displayed prominently in the Smithsonian Institute in Washington, D. C.

Chick introduced me to Benny Goodman, who in turn, asked me to write some arrangements for his then-band vocalist, Frances Hunt, who joined the band in early 1937, but only stayed for a few months. I don't recall what I had written for her, but I do remember also writing an instrumental arrangement of "Mean to Me" for the band. Benny never recorded the things I arranged, but knowing that he liked my stuff well enough to play them was a big enough honor for me.

The year also saw Chick engaged in a number of band battles at the Savoy. On February 28 he was against Fletcher Henderson, who came out of "retirement" as a bandleader after writing some renowned and stellar pieces for Benny Goodman; against Duke Ellington on March 7 (which Chick lost); and on May 11 against Benny, the "King of Swing" himself. The Webb-Goodman battle was one of the greatest events of the Swing Era. The event was billed as "The Musical Battle of the Century" and "Savoy's Greatest Event." And it certainly was! I know, because I was there.

Benny, just 27 years old, was riding high on the crest of popularity. His band was the top band in the country at the time. Two months earlier he had finished a memorable two-week engagement at the Paramount Theater that caused quite a stir—large crowds lined up around the block daily for hours hoping to gain entrance and bobby-sockers danced to his music in the theater aisles. His sojourn to the Savoy immediately came off the heels of a successful stint in the Madhattan Room of the Hotel Pennsylvania in New York.

Benny was packing dynamite with Harry James, Ziggy Elman and Chris Griffin on trumpets; Red Ballard and Murray McEachern on trombones; Hymie Shertzer, George Koenig, Art Rollini and Vido Musso in the sax section; Jess Stacy on piano; Allan Reuss, guitar; Harry Goodman on string bass; and, of course, Gene Krupa on drums.

Chick carried high explosives of his own with Mario Bauza, Bobby Stark and Taft Jordan on trumpets; Sandy Williams and Nat Story on trombones; Pete Clark, Louie Jordan, Teddy McRae and Wayman Carver in the sax section; Tommy Fulford on piano; John Trueheart, guitar; Beverly Peer on string bass; with the Maestro himself on drums.

On that Tuesday, May 11, evening more than four thousand swing fans, having paid the rather-pricey one-dollar admission fee, crowded the Savoy, breaking an attendance record, while another estimated five thousand lined Lenox Avenue, tying up traffic for hours. The fire department, riot squad, mounted police, and reserves were all called out to help keep order. It was quite a sight. It looked like a mini-version of Times Square on New Year's Eve, only more compact.

While most band battles were nothing more than a public relations ploy to generate dancer interest and excitement, for Chick this was the real deal. He was a fierce competitor and took such affairs very seriously. He considered the Savoy his own personal territory, to be defended against all invaders. He may have also felt that he had something to prove because of his physical condition. Who knows? But on this particular night Chick had a "take-no-prisoners" mindset against Benny.

He had good reasons. When Benny started his brand-new band in 1934, he brought his men to the Savoy hoping they would play with the same kind of "guts" that Chick's men employed. In so doing, Benny's band succeeded brilliantly with music that closely resembled that of the little drummer. Plus, Edgar Sampson had given Benny some of Chick's biggest hits, including "Stompin' at the Savoy" and "If Dreams Come True" (and later "Don't Be That Way") while his own band struggled to make such charts commercial successes. Nor was Chick pleased that Benny had "borrowed" Ella for a recording session six months earlier just as Ella's growing popularity was bringing Chick some overdue recognition. Chick also found it difficult to accept that Gene Krupa, who learned much from him, was widely regarded as the best drummer in the country. So this was really going to be a showdown between these two eminent traps artists.

Chick held intense afternoon rehearsals days before in preparation for this battle. He wanted everything precise and perfect. He told the guys in the band the night before, "Fellas, tomorrow is *my* hour. Anybody that misses notes, don't come back to work!"

Situated on the left bandstand, Benny started things off with his opening theme, "Let's Dance," immediately followed by the Harry James flag-waver "Peckin'," and the crowd went wild. Chick and crew, positioned on the right bandstand, responded with their set with Chick going full bore on the drums, which worked the crowd to a fevered pitch.

Everybody was swinging and I thought the floor was going to collapse at one point. Thank God it never did.

Benny regrouped during the intermission and opened the second set with a rousing Jimmy Mundy arrangement of "Jam Session," a huge crowd pleaser. Chick then responded with his own version of the same tune, which brought the house down. The grin on Chick's face told the whole story. He knew he had won.

There were different opinions as to who actually came out on top that night. The popular consensus was that Chick out-swung Benny and therefore, won hands down. Even the headline in the June 1937 issue of *Metronome* shouted "Chick Webb Defeats Ben Goodman!"

I personally thought it was a toss up. As far as individual musicianship goes, I thought Benny had the better band. But Chick's band had a spirit that night that was unbeatable. Teddy McRae was quoted later as saying, "Nobody could have taken it away from Chick that night." Even a heavily perspired Gene Krupa said that evening that a better man cut him. He was honest. But regardless of who won or who lost, it was truly a night to savor and a night I'll never forget. Both bands blew the roof off the Savoy and both groups were at the top of their games. For my money, both Chick and Benny co-reigned as "The *Kings* of Swing."

On a personal note…as the year 1937 came to a close, I received a small but nice write up in the December issue of *Metronome* about my working with the Chick Webb (and Benny Goodman) band. In addition, the magazine printed my special arrangement of that holiday favorite, "Jingle Bells." I took it as quite an honor to be recognized as such by one of the music businesses' leading trade publications.

While Chick's band was increasing in popularity, it would be another full year before it would become a household name. That would come as a result of a collaborative effort between Ella and me in taking a simple 60-year-old nursery rhyme and ultimately turning it into a mega-hit in its day.

CHAPTER FOUR

A-TISKET, A-TASKET

Nineteen-thirty-eight was looking to be very promising for Chick, Ella, and the band. It ended up being a fantasic year as Chick and company were catapulted into national stardom.

Chick started the new year off with a bang by engaging himself in another Battle of the Bands showdown. This time it was against William "Count" Basie and his swinging crew. Count Basie made his music sound so effortless. Each member of his stellar group was a fabulous soloist in his own right. In the trumpet section at the time was a young horn player named Harry "Sweets" Edison, with whom I had developed an enduring friendship over the years, right up until the time he passed away in 1999.

Handling the vocal duties for the Basie band were portly blues shouter Jimmy Rushing, known as "Mister Five by Five," and the fabulous Billie Holiday—"Lady Day" herself—who had joined the band for a brief tour a few months earlier.

This battle between Chick and Count Basie took place on Sunday, January 16, 1938. I wasn't there for this battle as I was at home sick with the flu. According to *Metronome*, Chick came out the winner that evening while *Down Beat* gave it to Basie. What made this battle so notable was it was the first time these two *grand dames* of jazz—Ella and Billie—were "competing" against each other at the same venue. According to that same *Down Beat* article, "Ella…was well out in front of Billie Holiday and James Rushing… Ella Fitzgerald caused a sensation with her rendition of 'Loch Lomand,' and Billie Holiday thrilled fans with 'My Man.' When Ella sang, she had the whole crowd rocking with her." I heard later that it was one helluva show. I'm only sorry that I missed it.

In February, Chick and the band were booked for a five-week stay at the Flamingo Room located on the second floor of Levaggi's Restaurant on Route 28 in North Reading, Massachusetts, just 20 miles north of Boston. It was a classy establishment and also a popular hangout for the college kids expecially from nearby Harvard University. Business in that area was in a slump, but during Chick's stay business exploded. The "King of the Drums" and his Savoy musical contingency caused a sensation.

Ella's version of my arrangement of "Rock it For Me" hit the charts that month and, coupled with the large crowds that came to hear the band, Chick's stay at Levaggi's was extended to May 2. The band was also broadcasting shows coast-to-coast from the restaurant three times a week and was getting fabulous write-ups in the music magazines. *Down Beat* called Ella the "First Lady of Swing," the first time her nickname appeared in print.

During his stint at Levaggi's, Chick's physical health began to worsen. On April 4, he was admitted to the hospital for two weeks. His friend, a guy named Scrippy, substituted for him on drums. Chick finished out the Levaggi's gig, but was always physically exhausted afterwards.

I was making the 225-mile trek from New York to Boston by train every week to deliver my three arrangements. Because of all the publicity Ella and the band were receiving, naturally, all of the music publishers were after Chick to broadcast all the current hits. He was loading me up two or three weeks ahead of time with writing assignments.

Whenever Chick and the band went on the road, I usually waited for them to return to New York before delivering any new arrangements. If they had a "location" job where they stayed in one spot for three or four weeks, then I would mail the arrangements to Chick in care of the location. In this particular case, since Levaggi's wasn't that far away, I could personally deliver the charts to Chick.

When I could be with the band, I oversaw the rehearsals just to make certain that the tempos were correct and that there weren't any wrong notes on anyone's part. With the load of talent that Chick's band possessed, I really didn't have to lead any rehearsal. All I had to do was set the tempo and the band went on cruise control.

Ella usually rehearsed the new tunes separately with Tommy Fulford, our piano player, and he'd work out the proper key which was comfortable for her. That's the only preparation she did as she learned the music very quickly. Once she got the song down and heard my arrangement, it would be like magic the way she performed it.

One day when I arrived at Levaggi's, Ella said to me, "Al, I have a great idea for a song. Why don't you try to work up something on the old nursery rhyme 'A-Tisket, A-Tasket?'"

"Gee, that's a great idea, Ella, let me think about it," I replied.

Since Chick had given me assignments for the following two weeks—that was six tunes—the reality was, I just didn't have time to think about "A-Tisket, A-Tasket."

The following week Ella would ask me, "Did you think about it?"

"Yes, I thought about it, Ella, but I just didn't have the time to get to it this week," I said.

The next week, the same thing happened. I didn't get to it, and this time, Ella got a little testy, which she'd never done.

"Well, look, Al, if you don't want to do it or can't do it, I'll ask Edgar Sampson to do it because I think it's too good an idea to ..."

"Hold the phone, Ella!" I shot back. "I'll get to it next week. I promise."

You have to realize that "A-Tisket, A-Tasket" is an old nursery rhyme that's been in the public domain since 1879. There was never really a song; it was just a little rhythm thing that the kids used to sing.

The following night when I arrived home, I burned some midnight oil and worked on it. I put the piece into a 32-bar frame. I added the release (middle section), the bridge, and wrote all the novelty lyrics, including the dialog between Ella and the band where they sang *"Was it red? No, no, no, no. Was it blue? No, no, no, no."*

The next time I went to Levaggi's, I presented Ella with my long-delayed project. She was excited. We went over the arrangement and she loved it. But she wanted to change some of the lyrics. I had originally written in the middle part, *"She was **walkin'** on down the avenue, without a single thing to do,"* and Ella said, "Let's say 'She was **truckin'** on down the avenue.'" She thought that using the word "*truckin',*" which was a popular word in those days, would make the song a little more "hip" for 1938. I thought she was right, so I said, "Yes, great!"

In its final form, the lyrics went like this:

> *A-tisket a-tasket*
> *A green and yellow basket*
> *I sent a letter to my mommy*
> *And on the way I dropped it*

I dropped it, I dropped it
Yes, on the way I dropped it
A little girlie picked it up
And put it in her pocket

She was truckin' on down the avenue,
Without a single thing to do
She was peck-peck-peckin' all around
When she spied it on the ground

She took it, she took it
my little yellow basket
And if she doesn't bring it back
I think that I shall die

(Was it brown?) no, no, no, no,
(Was it red?) no, no, no, no,
(Was it blue?) no, no, no, no,
Just a little yellow basket

I rehearsed the song with Chick, Ella, and the band that afternoon as it was scheduled for the broadcast that evening. Leo Talent, a song plugger who worked for Robbins Music Corporation, was at the rehearsal. He got real excited about the song and called his boss, Abe Olman, in New York, and told him to "tape this thing [on acetate] off the air tonight and see what you think." Everyone who listened to the broadcast that evening, including Olman and all the bigwigs at Robbins Music, raved about "A-Tisket, A-Tasket."

Two weeks later, on May 2—my 23rd birthday, incidentally—Chick and Ella went into the Decca recording studios in New York to wax the song, along with three other pieces, including my instrumental arrangement of "Azure." On that recording session was Mario Bauza, Bobby Stark and Taft Jordan, trumpets; Nat Story, Sandy Williams, and George Matthews, trombones; Garvin Bushnell, Hilton Jefferson, Teddy McRae and Wayman Carver, saxophones; Tommy Fulford, piano; Bobby Johnson, guitar; Beverly Peer, bass; and Chick, of course, on drums.

Even though there was an air of expectancy by music executives about "A-Tisket, A-Tasket," I had no idea what to expect when we went to record it. Recording music is much like the game of roulette, using ten-inch 78RPM platters as the chips. Sometimes the songs that you think are going to turn out big don't; and the tunes that seem innocuous, ironically, turn out to be the blockbusters.

When "A-Tisket, A-Tasket" was released a few weeks later, Lady Luck was on our side. The record broke big. It was number ten on June 18 and hit number one the first week in July. It became the nation's number one hit song that summer, staying at that position on the *Lucky Strike Hit Parade* radio show for nineteen consecutive weeks. It was an indescribable feeling to hold that fragile 78RPM platter in my hands and to read "Al Feldman and Ella Fitzgerald" printed in gold lettering against a blue background on Decca's label as co-composers of "A-Tisket, A-Tasket."

The first time "A-Tisket, A-Tasket" made its way into the movies was in the 1940 film *The Grapes of Wrath*, starring Henry Fonda. Ella sang it two years later in the Abbott and Costello musical comedy, *Ride 'Em Cowboy*. It was reintroduced in the 1944 film, *Two Girls and a Sailor*, starring Van Johnson, June Allyson, and Gloria DeHaven. It eventually became a million-seller twelve years after it was originally recorded.

"A-Tisket, A-Tasket" continues to find its way onto more contemporary recordings, thus introducing new generations of listeners to the song. The multi-Grammy Award-winning jazz vocal group the Manhattan Transfer did it a few years back, and jazz violinist Regina Carter recorded a version of it on her 2006 CD, *I'll Be Seeing You: A Sentimental Journey*. Other versions were also done by Patti Austin, Dee Dee Bridgewater, and actor/singer Mandy Patinkin. In addition, a more updated arrangement of the song recently provided the musical backdrop for competitive celebrity dancing on the hit televison show, *Dancing with the Stars*.

Because "A-Tisket, A-Tasket" was such an enormous hit, it helped to firmly establish Chick and Ella—and me, to some extent—in the business. The band broke attendance records everywhere it went. All throughout the summer of 1938, as a publicity ploy, "A-Tisket, A-Tasket" contests were held everywhere the band played. Little girls were dressed up and prizes were given away as to who sang "A-Tisket, A-Tasket" the best.

The real irony of this story is as a result of "A-Tisket, A-Tasket," Ella, Chick and I were inducted into the Grammy Hall of Fame in 1986 as part of the National Academy of Recording Arts and Sciences' way of honoring recordings of "lasting qualitative or historical significance that are at least 25 years old." It was a big honor. Chick was just starting to make it right at the height of the song's popularity, but, unfortunately, he didn't last long enough. He was quite ill and was unable to really cash in on "A-Tisket, A-Tasket." If I hadn't written the song, Edgar Sampson or somebody else would have ended up doing it. It was Ella's idea. I'm just grateful and lucky that I found the time to do it.

After "A-Tisket, A-Tasket" was recorded, the band went on to play for a week's stay at the Apollo Theater and on May 29 appeared as one of a number of swing outfits at the packed Randall's Island Stadium on the East River in New York City for a massive outdoor swing session. The celebrated event was hosted by Martin Block to benefit unemployed musicians.

In the ensuing weeks and months, Chick and company suddenly found themselves as the "IT" band and were now playing a number of upscale white-only establishments, thanks to Moe Gale, Chick's manager. In September, Chick set an attendance record at the Paramount Theater, breaking a five-year all-white record. Up until that time, Chick was only the third black band ever to play the Paramount, following Louis Armstrong and Cab Calloway. Later, Chick played a very successful engagement in the exclusive, all-white Cocoanut Grove of the Park Central Hotel on Broadway in New York.

I had the opportunity of going on a few short road trips with the band during this period and I got quite an education, to say the least. Travelling on the bus the guys seemed more relaxed, more fraternity-oriented, if you will. There was a lot of joking around as well as ongoing poker or crap games at the back of the bus. It was on the bus that I was first introduced to pot smoking, which I knew nothing about. It was the first time that I was exposed to it. Although I was around it, I never tried it. I saw the results of its effects of rowdiness and high-temperment and decided that wasn't for me. I was the only white guy in and around the band outside of Chick's manager and Frank Herz, the band's road manager. The guys in the band used to call us white guys "*ofays.*" It's Pig Latin—where the initial consonant sound of an English word is placed at the end and an *ay* is affixed—for "foe": f-o-e.

While racism was a boil that was prevalent on America's rear end at that time, I never felt any racial divide at all with members of Chick's band. If anything was there, I wasn't cognizant of it. As a matter of fact, the guys were really wonderful to me, and I have some wonderful memories and pleasantries of being with the guys and having a glass of wine with them, and so forth, after rehearsals.

When Chick first hired me to be one of his arrangers, my parents weren't too happy about it. They couldn't see anything good come of me hanging around black musicians. But when they saw that I had a future, they sort of came over to my side. I must admit it was a little unusual for a white kid to have spent so much time in Harlem, but I didn't care. I was colorblind. I just wanted to be near the music. It didn't matter to me the color of the person's skin that was making it.

One of the musicians in Chick's band that I got to know pretty well was trumpeter Taft Jordan. Taft was a fun-loving guy who blew really hot solos, often trading main trumpet soloist duties with Bobby Stark. Taft played early in his career with the Washboard Rhythm Kings before joining Chick's orchestra in 1933, remaining there until 1942 while Ella was the band's frontwoman. From 1943 to 1947, he played with Duke Ellington, then with Lucille Dixon at the Savannah Club in New York City from 1949 to 1953. He toured with Benny Goodman in 1958, played on Miles Davis' *Sketches of Spain* album (1960), and worked with the New York Jazz Repertory Company. He recorded four tunes as a leader in 1935, and led his own band in 1960-61, recording a number of albums. Taft died in New York in 1981, at age 65.

One vivid memory I have of Taft turned out to be for him a life-changing moment of which I inadvertently played a part. This was a classic case of "watch what you say." The situation had such meaning for Taft that he shared it with Stanley Dance as an anecdote in his book, *The World of Swing*. While Taft was a gifted soloist, he always wanted to try his hand at playing lead trumpet. The lead trumpet player in Chick's band was Mario Bauza. Taft used to ask Chick all the time if he could play lead as well as jazz solo, but Chick would always put him off on the idea. Finally, one day in 1938, Chick called an impromptu rehearsal but Mario Bauza was at Yankee Stadium taking in a Yankees game and he was nowhere to be found. Everyone in the band was waiting for Mario to return. While Chick was outside getting some air, I suggested to the guys in the band to let Taft try the lead part. I kicked off the tempo on the next piece and Chick came running back in wanting to know who was playing lead trumpet. I told Chick that it was Taft. Chick wanted to start the arrangement again from the top. He liked what he heard. From then on, Chick gave Taft double-duty, gradually giving him more lead to play, while maintaining his jazz soloist chair.

Another memory that stands out about Taft involved him and me engaging in some playful fisticuffs antics. During a break at the Decca recording studios, Taft and I were fooling around boxing each other. I don't know how it happened, but he walked into my right jab and it caught him on the jaw and he fell down. He wasn't hurt, thank goodness, and we all laughed about it. It became a standing joke with Taft and me for many years. As a matter of fact, Butch Stone used to say to people, "Don't fool around with Van. You know what he did to Taft Jordan!"

When people hear that I worked for Chick Webb, they inveriably ask me about Louie Jordan, a star performer with Chick who became known later as "The King of the Jukebox" for his many jump blues hits he recorded with his group, "The Tympany Five." Louie started off his career playing with Clarence Williams and then with Charlie Gaines. During the summer of 1936 he was invited to join Chick's outfit. The ebullient Louie was quite a showman and his performances were a major attraction with the band. Louie and Ella often duetted on stage and they would later reprise the partnership on several records, such as their 1946 chart-toppers, "Stone Cold Dead in the Market" and "Petootie Pie," by which time both artists were major stars.

The fact is, I really didn't have much close contact with Louie while he was with the band. He pretty much went off and did his own thing. He was, however, very affable and very complimentary on the things I did for him. One of the novelty songs that I arranged for Louie that he did for stage shows was "Mayor of Alabam." It was a great crowd pleaser. The guys in the band loved it as well and they would later call Louie "Mayor."

It was reputed that Louie and Ella had a thing going at one time. Some speculated it was a romance, but it seemed to be strickly business. He was trying to convince Ella and other band members to leave Chick to join the new band he was forming. That didn't sit too well with Chick, so, in the spring of 1938, he gave Louie his walking papers. That didn't seem to effect Louie's career one iota, as he went on to score 58 hit singles between 1942 and 1951 with such classics as "Caldonia," "Let the Good Times Roll," "I'm Gonna Move to the Outskirts Of Town," "What's the Use of Getting Sober (When You're Gonna Get Drunk Again)," "Ain't Nobody Here But Us Chickens," and "Choo Choo Ch'Boogie," among others. It's a no-brainer that in 2004, *Rolling Stone* ranked him Number 59 on their list of the "100 Greatest Artists of All Time." Louie died in 1975, at age 67.

Teddy McRae, another standout in Chick's band, was the band's main tenor sax soloist. He also did some arranging. Before he joined Chick in early 1936, Teddy's musical associations included Elmer Snowden, Stuff

Smith and Lil Armstrong. Teddy remained with the band after Chick's death, acting as the musical director for a period while the group was fronted by Ella. He later had stints with the orchestras of Cab Calloway, Jimmie Lunceford, Lionel Hampton, and Louis Armstrong, being Louis' musical director during 1944-45. He wrote "Back Bay Shuffle" for Artie Shaw before leading his own band in 1945. Teddy died in 1999, at age 91.

Like Louie Jordan, I didn't know Teddy McRae that well. In his comments about the Chick Webb band, Teddy was quoted in one publication as saying, "Chick took a liking to a young white arranger who tried to change our musical syle. He came to the band with a lot of new arranging ideas, using modern chords." That white arranger Teddy was referring to was me. He sort of put me down a little for changing the syle of the band. Actually, when I did all the things for Ella, which were all pop tunes, that indeed changed the style of the band. It's what *Chick* wanted. Chick was honing in on a more commercial sound for the band's star attraction, which was Ella.

While Chick knew what he wanted from his band, he was primarily a musician and not a P.R. person. To help build a more intimate rapport with his listeners, he hired Bardu Ali, a very handsome and suave musician whose mother hailed from New Orleans and his father from Arabia, to act as the band's frontman. Bardu was very capable in his role as master of ceremonies. Before joining Chick, Bardu was involved with the black cinema. In 1940, Bardu formed his own band, and made his way to Los Angeles where he presided as the master of ceremonies at the Lincoln Theater on Central Avenue. He then became the business partner for rhythm-and-blues pianist and preacher Johnny Otis, performing in Otis's band and opening the famous Barrelhouse Club with him. He later became comedian Redd Foxx's business manager.

In fact, Bardu played in an episode on Foxx's hit comedy series, *Sanford and Son*. Bardu played the role of an impending bride's father in "Here Comes the Bride, There Goes the Bride," which aired over NBC on January 28, 1972. Foxx did Bardu wrong during the course of their association together and the two separated as bad friends.

My association with Bardu was very close. I hadn't seen him for many years after I left Chick's band. We bumped into each other in California when I was working at NBC. He was with Redd Foxx at the time. We reminisced about the old days. I asked him if he ever went back to visit Harlem.

"Yes, once in a while," he said, "but it's not very safe to walk around there these days." With that, he put his hand into his pocket and pulled out a small revolver, which looked like a starter's pistol.

"I always carry this whenever I'm walking up Lenox Avenue," he added. "If a guy stops me or two guys stop me and ask, 'Hey, Buddy, got a match?' I pull out this thing and tell them, 'This is the only match I have.' Then they split."

I didn't see Bardu again after that all-too-brief chance reunion. He died in 1981, at age 75, and I attended his funeral here in Los Angeles.

It's funny how one song can make celebrities out of persons literally overnight and subsequently make anything else they record become minor hits. Such was the case with Chick and Ella. After "A-Tisket, A-Tasket," a handful of songs which I arranged for Ella hit the charts later that year. "I Found My Yellow Basket," the immediate follow-up to "A-Tisket, A-Tasket," shot up to number three, "Wacky Dust" at thirteen, and "MacPherson Is Rehearsin' (To Swing)" at fourteen. "F.D.R. Jones," from the Broadway musical *Sing Out the News*, soon followed, reaching at number eight.

More hits kept coming. The following spring, Chick and Ella's version of "Undecided" (recorded on February 17, 1939) was on the chart at number eight, followed by "'Taint What You Do" (also recorded on the same day) going for one week at nineteen, and Ella's composition of "Chew, Chew, Chew, Chew Your Bubble Gum" (recorded on March 2, 1939) charted for a week at fourteen. But by that time I was no longer with the band.

Of course, no one has to recap how Ella's career turned out. It's self-evident. Her star turned out to be the biggest and brightest of all who came out of the Chick Webb band. Ella was known as a singer's singer, with a beautiful tone, terrific range, and a great sense of rhythm, earning the respect and admiration of all who worked with her. Composer Ira Gershwin once said, "I never knew how good our songs were until I heard Ella Fitzgerald sing them." And he was so right.

Ella's *Songbook* projects—of such composers as Cole Porter, Harold Arlen, Irving Berlin, Duke Ellington, George and Ira Gershwin, Jerome Kern, Richard Rodgers and Lorenz Hart, and Johnny Mercer—rank as some of the most ambitious and definitive works that were ever undertaken.

After I had moved out to California, I did a few arrangements for Ella's nightclub acts and theater dates. Ray Brown, her husband at the time, called me and asked me to write some things for her, which I was more than happy to do.

I must admit that it bothered me for quite some time that I didn't have a chance to work with Ella on any of her *Songbook* albums. I didn't blame her at all. She really had no say in who worked with her on these projects. They were all Norman Granz's productions. He was personally managing her career at the time. He never dug me for some reason or another. I probably could have gone to Ella for old-time's sake and asked her to let me come aboard and she would have gone to bat for me, but I didn't want to go over Norman's head. I didn't want to open a can of worms by doing that, so I never persued it. Besides, I was very busy doing TV and film work, so I let those negative thoughts about that situation go.

Over the years Ella and I kept in pretty close contact with each other. When I served as President of the Los Angeles Chapter of the National Academy for Recording Arts and Sciences (NARAS), I had the distinction of presenting Ella with her seventh Grammy Award in 1962 for "Best Solo Performance by a Female" for her album, *Ella Swings Brightly with Nelson Riddle.* She was working at the Flamingo Hotel in Las Vegas at the time and wasn't able to attend the Grammy ceremonies. The NARAS Committee suggested I go to Las Vegas to present Ella with her special award. It was wonderful for me to share such a celebrative moment with her.

Over the years, Ella won 13 Grammy Awards and many other honors, including the National Medal of Arts, presented to her in 1987 by President Ronald Reagan. In 1989, The Society of Singers created a special award named after Ella called the ELLA Award, to honor singers chosen for their contribution to the music world and for their dedicated efforts to benefit the community and worldwide humanitarian causes.

During the last few years of her life Ella suffered serious complications from diabetes and had to have both her legs amputated below the knees, confining her to a wheelchair. Naturally, I was very saddened to hear of her passing on June 15, 1996, at age 79. I attended her funeral in Beverly Hills. The music world lost a much-beloved artistic treasure and I lost a dear friend.

On January 10, 2007, I was thrilled to hear the announcement by the United States Postal Service that Ella would be honored with her own 39-cent postage stamp which would be released that coming April. The stamp was part of the Postal Service's Black Heritage series.

I thought Ella was certainly deserving of such a wonderful honor—an honor that, in my opinion, was way overdue. On the day that the Ella stamp first came out, I went to the local post office to purchase them in bulk. Being in a facetious mood, I told the postal clerk that Ella and I were partners on a big song once and that I thought my picture should be on the stamp with her. He said, "You wouldn't want your picture on there. You have to be *dead* in order to have your picture on a U.S. postage stamp." That put me straight! So much for equal billing…

If Ella were alive, I believe she would have been happy about receiving such an honor, but she wouldn't have made a big deal about it. She just wasn't that way. Ella was a very humble person who was rather shy and very private. She was that way when I first met her and as the years went on, she hadn't changed one iota. I don't think she ever realized how great she really was.

Even the late great composer, arranger, bandleader, and multi-instrumentalist Benny Carter echoed that same sentiment when he once said, "Ella has no great ego, no sense of having accomplished all she has."

I believe Ella will be remembered for her voice, her diction, and her intonation. Everything was just perfect. She was like a wonderful instrumentalist with her voice. Her records will live on forever. For my money, there will never be another Ella.

By the same token, there will never be another Chick Webb. Chick was a pioneer and master of the drums. He influenced countless drummers with his musical taste and rhythmic sensibilities.

He led one of the greatest, yet underrated, musical aggregations to ever come out of the Swing Era. While Benny Goodman is credited with ushering in the Swing Era, Chick was doing it a few years before Benny. The trouble was, no one was paying any attention. Chick knew he had a great band and he wanted the world to know it as well. He poured his whole life into music, tirelessly working on improving the band's sound and identity. Chick's motto had always been "Music comes first." And he lived by his creed.

Chick was always very kind, very supportive, and very appreciative of what I was doing for the band. He was not just my boss, but in many respects, he was a friend and an older brother all rolled into one. He and his wife, Sallie, invited me a number of times to their apartment on "Striver's Row" on West 138th Street for dinner. Chick was always so arrangement-conscious. He'd always talk to me about arrangements. Every nickel that he got, he bought new arrangements for the band. He'd play records whenever I came over and he would become so enthused at what certain soloists were doing on these recordings. His whole life was his band and making it a success.

Although critics have second-guessed Chick's decision from going from a strictly jazz-oriented format to a more commercial set-up, Chick knew what he was doing. He was crazy like a fox. Even though some members of his band may have thought he was selling out, in reality, he was just *selling*. He saw a marketing value in Ella that would bring his band broader appeal and wider recognition. He played a hunch and it worked.

The tragedy about it, though, was that Chick didn't live long enough to really enjoy the fruits of his labors. Just as Chick, Ella and the band were riding high on the crest of "A-Tisket, A-Tasket" and the other chart-toppers that followed, Chick's failing health was becoming more pronounced. He was experiencing great pain in his spine, thus limiting his playing at live performances.

In April 1939, Chick was in such terrible pain that he entered Johns Hopkins Hospital in Baltimore for treatment. Doctors operated on him, draining fluid in his back. After a few weeks in the hospital, Chick was well enough to be discharged. In early May the band did a brief stint at the Southland Café in Boston. Airchecks from the thirty-minute May 4 radio broadcast have enjoyed reissue by record collectors.

Following the Southland Café booking, the band headed down the East Coast doing a string of grueling one-nighters. Chick was getting worse with each booking. In Washington, D.C., Chick left to return to Johns Hopkins Hospital in Baltimore. He was having problems with his kidneys as well as his ongoing difficulties with his spine. After another operation, he died quietly in his hospital room on June 16, 1939, with his mother, wife, and a few relatives by his side. His last words on this side of eternity were, "I'm sorry, I gotta go!" Chick was only 30 years old.

Back in the fall of 1938, I left Chick to form my own band. I was playing at the Roseland Ballroom in New York when news reached me of Chick's passing. On the remote broadcast from the Roseland, I expressed sincere condolences to Sallie and the rest of Chick's family. I was heartbroken. I loved that little man tremendously.

I, along with my wife, Beth, attended Chick's funeral a few days later at Waters African Methodist Episcopal Church on North Aisquith Street in Baltimore. Over 1,200 family, friends, and musicians crammed themselves into the tiny church sanctuary to pay their final respects. The sweltering temperatures inside the church, coupled with Baltimore's intense summer heat and humidity on the outside, made the two-hour service just barely doable. There wasn't a dry eye in the church.

Another estimated 8,000 to 10,000 mourners crowded the immediate block outside the church, causing traffic headaches for local law enforcement officials. Many climbed rooftops of buildings or straddled ridgepoles of houses in order the catch a final glimpse of this musical giant, their local boy who made good. Newspaper reports called the event "the largest funeral turnout in recent history."

Members of Chick's band were set to play a special piece of music during the service, but couldn't as their grief was all-consuming. Ella was barely able to compose herself long enough to sing two choruses of "My Buddy," sobbing uncontrollably afterwards. Teddy McRae played "End of a Perfect Day" accompanied by Tommy Fulford who played straight piano while wiping the tears that were streaming down his face with his left hand.

Tribute messages came from a host of swing's greatest musicians, including Cab Calloway, Duke Ellington, Earl Hines, Louis Armstrong, Gene Krupa, Davey Tough, Teddy Hill, Fletcher Henderson, Erskine Hawkins, Claude Hopkins, Willie Bryant, and Roy Eldridge, among others. Fletcher Henderson, Benny Carter, and Al Cooper (the Savoy Sultans) were active pallbearers, while Duke Ellington, Cab Calloway, Jimmie Lunceford and Gene Krupa were named honorary pallbearers

As Chick's body lay in state at the Webb house on Ashland Avenue and later in the church prior to the formal services, an estimated 15,000 mourners passed by the Little Drummer's bier.

As I sat there during the service I couldn't help but think that all Chick wanted was to be successful in music. If the throngs of people who attended his funeral were any indication of that success, then his goal was achieved, albeit in somewhat of a perverse way. Despite the validity of that thought or not, all I knew at that moment was that beaming smile and infectious boyhood grin that Chick always displayed while playing drums would be no more.

Writer Richard S. Ginell summed up Chick's life beautifully when he wrote, "Chick Webb represented the triumph of the human spirit in jazz and life." Amen to that!

After Chick's passing, Ella fronted the band, calling it "Ella Fitzgerald and Her Famous Orchestra." This started Ella's career as a bandleader, one of the few female bandleaders in a business that at the time was dominated by males. Ella had mild success at band leadership, but the band itself never really took off. In 1942, Ella disbanded and went on to focus on a solo career, while the orchestra that Chick Webb once organized faded into memory.

It's a sobering thought for me to realize now that I'm in my "twilight years," that I'm the lone surviving member of the Chick Webb Orchestra. All the principle players who made Chick's music so wonderfully exciting have all, as we say in the music business, "taken a cab." In memorium are listed here some of those departed personnel: Bobby Stark, 39, trumpeter, December 29, 1945; John Trueheart, 49, guitarist/banjoist, 1949; Tommy Fulford, 44, pianist, December 16, 1956; Claude Jones, 60, trombonist, January 17, 1962; Elmer Williams, 57, saxophonist/clarinetist, June 1962; Moe Gale, 66, manager of Chick Webb, September 1964; Hilton Jefferson, saxophonist, November 14, 1968; Pete Clarke, saxophonist/clarinetist, March 27, 1975; Charles Buchanan, 86, manager of the Savoy Ballroom, December 1984; Chauncy Haughton, 80, saxophonist/clarinetist, July 1, 1989; Eddie Barefield, 81, saxophonist/clarinetist/arranger, January 3, 1991; Sandy Williams, 84, trombonist, March 25, 1991; Garvin Bushell, 89, saxophonist/clarinetist, October 31, 1991; Mario Bauza, 82, trumpeter, July 11, 1993; and Beverly Peer, 84, bassist, January 16, 1997.

While "A-Tisket, A-Tasket" helped to put Chick and Ella "on the map," so to speak, it afforded me some recognition as well. I was now invited by a record executive to venture out into the music world donning a new hat—that of a bandleader.

Right: Chick Webb, "The King of the Drums." He was my first boss as well as my mentor and friend. Chick may have been a small man, but he had a big heart.

Left: Ella performing in front of the Chick Webb band in 1937. Chick is playing the drums while perched high above the rest of the crew. Also pictured to the right is baritone saxophonist Chauncey Haughton.

Above: Chick Webb and his Orchestra in Chicago during the summer of 1937. (Back row, L-R) are: Wayman Carver, tenor saxophone/flute; Bill Johnson, guitar; Tommy Fulford, piano; Taft Jordan, trumpet; Nat Story and Sandy Williams, trombones; Bardu Ali, Master of Ceremonies; Teddy McRae, tenor sax; and Chauncey Haughton, alto saxophone. (Front row, L-R) are: Mario Bauza, trumpet; Beverly Peer, string bass; Chick Webb, drums/leader; Louis Jordan, alto saxophone; and Charlie Linton, vocalist.

Right: One of many posters advertising the Chick Webb Orchestra with its feature attraction Ella Fitzgerald at the Savoy Ballroom in Harlem. Chick's was the house band at the Savoy for many years.

Left: Ella out in front of the crowd in Asbury Park, New Jersey, while Bardu Ali, the Chick Webb band's front man, looks on.

Below: The marquee outside the Paramount Theater in New York City in September 1938 advertising the appearance of the Chick Webb Band with Ella Fitzgerald. Chick set an attendance record at the Paramount, breaking a five-year all-white record. Up until that time, Chick was only the third black band ever to play at the renowned theater.

Left: Neon lights above the entrance to the Savoy Ballroom bidding patrons welcome into the "World's Finest Ball Room."

Left: Lindy Hoppers dancing on "The Track" at the Savoy Ballroom.

Right: All that remains today on the original site of the Savoy Ballroom is this plaque commemorating the famed nightspot's cultural significance. The Savoy Ballroom still holds lots of happy memories for me.

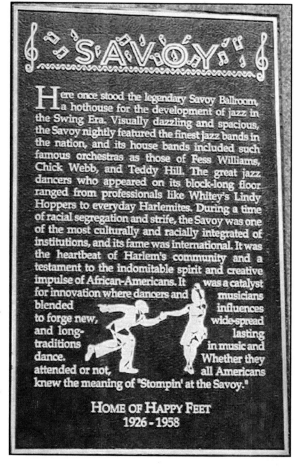

♪ SAVOY ♪

Here once stood the legendary Savoy Ballroom, a hothouse for the development of jazz in the Swing Era. Visually dazzling and spacious, the Savoy nightly featured the finest jazz bands in the nation, and its house bands included such famous orchestras as those of Fess Williams, Chick Webb, and Teddy Hill. The great jazz dancers who appeared on its block-long floor ranged from professionals like Whitey's Lindy Hoppers to everyday Harlemites. During a time of racial segregation and strife, the Savoy was one of the most culturally and racially integrated of institutions, and its fame was international. It was the heartbeat of Harlem's community and a testament to the indomitable spirit and creative impulse of African-Americans. It was a catalyst for innovation where dancers and musicians blended influences to forge new, wide-spread and long- lasting traditions in music and dance. Whether they attended or not, all Americans knew the meaning of "Stompin' at the Savoy."

HOME OF HAPPY FEET
1926 - 1958

Above: A poster advertising the famed showdown between the Benny Goodman and Chick Webb bands at the Savoy Ballroom. This spectacular event was billed as "The Musical Battle of the Century." In many ways in was.

Left: A heavily perspired Gene Krupa grinning enthusiastically at the Savoy Ballroom during the big battle between the Benny Goodman and Chick Webb bands. Also pictured are fellow Goodman band members Harry Goodman, bass, left, and trumpeter Harry James, right.

Above: A Sunday afternoon jam session: Commodore Music Shop owner Milt Gabler, keeling, brought Chick Webb (left), Artie Shaw (middle), and Duke Ellington (right) at the Brunswick recording studios in New York in March 1937 for a series of free Sunday afternoon jam sessions. Standing in the crowd enjoying the music is jazz journalist and producer Helen Oakley Dance (light colored dress). Yours truly is at the far left wall with a big grin on his face. This photograph is now displayed prominently in the Smithsonian Institute in Washington, D. C.

Left: The record and song that made it all happen for me: A sheet music copy of Ben Cutler's version of "A-Tisket, A-Tasket" (left), and the original Decca recording of the same (below).

Below: When "A-Tisket, A-Tasket" was released during the summer of 1938, it became the nation's number one song staying on the *Lucky Strike Hit Parade* for nineteen weeks.

Above: Thousands of mourners came out in the sweltering heat and humidity to pay tribute to Chick Webb on the day of his funeral in June 1939 in Baltimore, Maryland. The Baltimore newspaper reports of the day called the event "the largest funeral turnout in recent history."

Left: Chick Webb sitting proudly at his drum set. Writer Richard S. Ginell summed up Chick's life beautifully when he wrote, "Chick Webb represented the triumph of the human spirit in jazz and life." He sure did!

Above: It was a proud moment for me as then-President of the Los Angeles Chapter of NARAS when I presented Ella her seventh Grammy Award in 1962 in Las Vegas. As a recording artist, Ella's voice, intonation, and diction were impeccable.

Left: The Ella stamp released by the U.S. Postal Service in April 2007. There will never be another Ella.

CHAPTER FIVE

AND THE BAND PLAYED ON

By the first week of July 1938, "A-Tisket, A-Tasket" catapaulted to number one on the charts and it seemed that "A-Tisket, A-Tasket"-mania was everywhere. All of us affiliated with the Chick Webb band were feeling elated that the tune was taking off the way it had. By the middle of the month I received an unexpected and surprise telephone call from Eli Oberstein, the head of RCA-Victor Records in New York.

Eli oversaw Victor Records, whose roster of bands at the time included Benny Goodman, Tommy Dorsey, Guy Lombardo, Bunny Berigan, and Fats Waller. Eli told me he was starting a stable of songwriting bandleaders for Victor's subsidiary label, Bluebird. He had gotten Larry Clinton and Les Brown to sign on and he wanted me to join the team. Because of "A-Tisket, A-Tasket," Eli thought I would produce a lot more hit songs.

Bluebird Records was originally created in 1932 to counter ARC Records in the "three records for a dollar" market. Along with ARC's Perfect Records, Melotone Records and Romeo Records, and the independent U.S. Decca label, Bluebird became one of the best-selling "cheap labels" of the 1930s and early 1940s. It was known as the 35-cent label. Shep Fields and his "Rippling Rhythm" Orchestra signed with the label as early as 1936. Two of the most popular swing bands of the late 1930s and early 1940s, Artie Shaw and Glenn Miller, were also Bluebird artists.

Eli made me an offer I couldn't refuse. My pay was to be $100 per week as an advance against all song royalties and money made with my new band. At the end of the year there would be an accounting and all overage monies would be split. He provided me with a record contract, and he would oversee my recording career to make sure everything would be fine. It sounded great to me, so I jumped right in.

When I told Chick the news, he wished me the best and much success. He was very gracious. It wasn't like I was leaving him; but rather, I was going out on a new venture of my own. I spent three wonderful years with Chick and I'll always be grateful to him for being my first "boss" and for giving me my start in the business.

Every band had a "band boy," a young guy who sets up the band-stand prior to an engagement and who handles the musical library for the band. Chick had a band boy whose name was "Pugh" (pronounced PEW). He was an enthusiastic young black man in his late teens. He and I developed a good rapport with each other. I never knew what his first name was because everyone just called him Pugh. When Pugh heard that I was leaving Chick to start my own band, he wanted to come with me to be my band boy.

"Well, what about Chick?" I asked.

"He has other guys he can get," Pugh said. "I want to go with you."

I didn't have a problem with Pugh joining my band, but I first discussed the matter over with Chick and he gave his blessings. So Pugh was my band boy for about the first six or eight months. Then Frank Herz, Chick's road manager, also came along with me, so I had a touch of the Chick Webb organization with me when I started out.

The first thing I did as a budding bandleader, even before I as-sembled any musicians, was to change my name. Eli said that the name "Al Feldman and his Orchestra" wouldn't sound too professional on a theater marquee. So, with the help of Eli's attorney, William Berkson, we brainstormed for a name change. I took the first part of my middle name, Van, and made it my first name. I then took my first name, Alexander, and made it my last name. I was now "Van Alexander." I liked the way it sounded and I then made the name-change legal in a court of law. From then on, I was known personally, professionally, and legally as Van Alexander.

Les Brown suggested to me that I get myself a manager. He recom-mended his manager, Joe Glaser, who was also representing Louis Armstrong at the time and who later managed Billie Holiday's career. Joe was an old "dese-and-dems-and-dose-guy" from Chicago. He was a rough guy and a wheeler-dealer. He had underworld dealings stemming from Prohibition-era days in Chicago with Al Capone and had connections for everything. I remember him telling me during World War II when rationing was practiced and certain items were hard to come by, "Don't worry, I can get you anything you want. If your wife wants silk stockings, I'll get her some silk stockings." Barring his somewhat dubious reputation, I felt that I was in good hands with Joe. I stayed with Joe until I came out to California in 1945 with Bob Crosby.

I wanted to emulate one of my favorite bands of all time: Isham Jones. His full, fat brass sound was always so distinctive. I always tried to have a good brass section. I was trying to concentrate on getting a good powerful lead trumpet player who could really front the brass section so that they would never be what I called "undernourished."

I immediately started to put a band together, which didn't take too long. I formed a neucleus of band personnel from my close friends from high school: Butch Stone on alto sax, Ray Barr on piano, and Roger Segan on drums. These three fellows then recommended other musicians to fill in the needed chairs to make up a fourteen-piece band.

Butch was the very first person I asked to join my new band. He was working a day job for Consolidated Films out of Fort Lee, New Jersey, delivering the latest movies to theaters in New York. He worked for a number of years with the Frank Rysen Orchestra, a local dance band, but Rysen disbanded in late 1936, and Butch continued playing locally wherever he could. I featured him a lot singing novelty tunes.

> "When Van asked me to be in his band, I enthusiastically agreed," said Butch Stone, 96. "He's my dearest friend and one of the nicest people who ever lived. Van had a really good band with all good musicians. It was a fun band, too!"

During our first year, Ray Barr played piano and I just conducted. Ray was a fabulous pianist who later worked with bandleader Vincent Lopez and singers Patti Page, Martha Raye, and Mary Martin before spending 21 years as Frankie Laine's accompanist. Ray died in 1983, at age 71.

Later on, I assumed the piano chair and I conducted the band from the piano. I was never a prolific piano player. I played what was called an "arranger's piano," mostly chords. I could make myself understood, but I was not a soloist.

Our original drummer was Roger Segan. He didn't work out and he stayed with the band until the end of January 1939 when Harry Fulterman replaced him.

I started building the band's library by writing lots of arrangements. When I got the personnel I wanted, we rehearsed intensively before presenting ourselves to the public. The initial line-up for my band included Bob Person, Milt Davidson, and Hy Small on trumpets; Jerry Rosa and Bill Schallenberger (later known as Bill Schallen) on trombones; Sol Kane and Butch Stone on alto saxes; Jack Greenberg and Harry Steinfeld on tenor saxes; Ray Barr, piano; Joel Livingston, guitar; George Hanrahan, bass; and Roger Segan, drums. Shirley Brown was our band vocalist.

Eli Oberstein had influence with booking agents and he got me to sign with Music Corporation of America (MCA), one of the biggest booking agencies around. My personal agent through MCA was Irving Lazar, who later became known as "Swifty" Lazar. He was one of the biggest dealmakers and literary agents for MCA. After putting together three major deals for Humphrey Bogart in a single day, he was dubbed "Swifty" by Bogart. The moniker stuck, but was a name he actually disliked. He died from cancer in 1993, at age 86.

MCA got us some pretty good jobs, not only on the road but also at regular places in the New York area such as The Top Hat in Union City, New Jersey. The Top Hat always provided airtime for us over the radio. We usually managed to get on the air at most places we played, which was vital for our exposure. We played The Steel Pier in Atlantic City, New Jersey; the prestigious Virginia Beach Club in Virginia Beach, Virginia; the outdoor bowl at Manhattan Beach, New York; and every other one-night stand from the top of New England down to the Carolinas to Upper Sandusky, Ohio, and as far west as Chicago.

Pennsylvania was a big place for us, especially the coal-mining towns, such Scranton, Allentown, and a place 80 miles west of Allentown called Shamokin. We played Shamokin, with a population at that time of about 18,000, during the winter. Dancers would come to where we were playing wearing big heavy boots and long coats. While coal miners had a reputation of being rowdy, we never experienced such behaviors and thus never had any problems with our coal-mining dancers.

One of our very first dates was a college prom at the posh Copley Plaza Hotel in Boston. The date almost ended in disaster for us. It would have, too, if it weren't for the fraternity of musicians coming to the aid of other musicians in times of crisis. Our bus met us at mid-morning at the Forrest Hotel in New York City, where we loaded the bus with our instruments, music and band equipment. We arrived at the Copley Plaza Hotel around four in the afternoon, in plenty of time for the gig.

Pugh set up the band in the ballroom where the prom was to be held. After finishing his task, he came to me with a worried look on his face and said, "Hey, Fess [he used to call me Fess, which was short for "Professor"], I think I left the first trumpet book in the lobby of the Forrest Hotel."

"You did *what?*" I responded in disbelief.

"Yeah, it's not here. I can't find it anywhere. I must have left it back there," he said.

What was I going to do? The first trumpet part was an absolute necessity. If it was the second or third trumpet part, we could get by, but we needed that first trumpet book if we were going to play our library.

I was in a panic. I then called Leighton Noble, an acquaintance of mine who was the bandleader at the Copley Plaza Hotel, and told him what had happened. He was quite understanding of my predicament. He then told me he had 100 stock arrangements of dance music available and that I would be welcomed to use them if I wanted.

With my back up against the wall and time running out, I took Leighton up on his kind and generous offer. Butch and a couple of the guys in the band and I got the stock arrangements and sorted through them by instrumentation to make books for each member of the band.

We played stock arrangements all night long for that prom date. Even Shirley Brown, our girl singer, "faked" her way beautifully through a handful of songs.

At the end of the evening, the dean of the college came over to me and said, "Mr. Alexander, I want to tell you that when we hired your band I heard that it was a loud jazz band, but your music tonight was delightful." I thought to myself, "So much for my arrangements."

The following day the first trumpet book was retrieved intact and we were able to play our style of music once again, much to my relief. That evening we were booked at Boston's Raymore-Playmore Ballroom, a twin ballroom that was uniquely separated by a walled partition. Two bands always played there at the same time, working simultaneously. Patrons couldn't hear one band from the other, but patrons could walk from one bandstand to the other through a hallway. The ballroom had a single price admission of 40 cents to hear both bands.

Performing in the other ballroom that night was Woody Herman and his wonderful "Band That Plays The Blues." Woody inherited the band from Isham Jones a few years earlier. It was here at the Raymore-Playmore that Butch debuted "A Good Man Is Hard to Find," an Eddie Green song that has long been associated with him. I had written an arrangement for him of this song, which perhaps more than any other tune, gave Butch his identity. When Butch did the song that night, he broke up the place.

> *"I guess the crowd [at the Raymore-Playmore] liked what I did because I got a rousing ovation afterwards,"* recalled Stone. *"The song turned out to be a good thing for me."*

In fact, every time and everywhere Butch did "A Good Man," he'd break up the place. When Butch left my band in 1940, he asked me if he could take the arrangement with him. I said, "Sure, you can have it. Nobody else can do it but you, anyhow." He continued to break up places with that song while with Jack Teagarden and then with Larry Clinton. He finally ended up with Les Brown, who had the foresight to record it in 1942. Why I never did, I don't know. Les' version of the tune sold something like a half-million copies. Les and I used to joke about the fact that I never got paid for my arrangement.

Just before Les passed away, he and I were playing golf and he said to me, "Guess what, Van? You're going to finally get paid for your arrangement of 'A Good Man Is Hard to Find.'"

"Oh, how come?" I asked.

"We're going to re-record it for the BASF label in Germany and they have to pay for all of the arrangements."

I guess patience is indeed a virtue, because 60 years later, I did indeed *finally* get paid for "A Good Man Is Hard to Find."

I developed a whole library of material for Butch. They were mostly comedy or entertainment tunes like "Hot Dog Joe," which I wrote especially for him. It was a *territorial* song about a hot dog vender. It was popular in New York but people in the South had no idea what Butch was singing about.

Our first big exposure was a radio appearance on *The Fitch Bandwagon*, a popular national hook-up radio show sponsored by the Fitch Hair Tonic Company. Many of the well-known bands of the day—both sweet and hot—clamored to get airtime on *The Fitch Bandwagon* radio show.

I had a few dollars in my pocket now and my future looked bright, so I thought it was a good time to tie the knot with Beth Baremore. Beth and I had been seeing each other since high school. But during the years after high school we each dated different people, but we found ourselves always coming back to each other. We had a mutual attraction for each other. We just found we'd rather be together than with other people.

My parents always adored Beth and got along famously with her. In fact, my father used to tell me that "Beth has a good head on her shoulders." Beth was intelligent and street-smart. She didn't drink or smoke.

While I was dating Beth, we'd go to the Savoy Ballroom lots of times to dance. She was a very good dancer. Beth just recently told me that she went alone to the Savoy to dance on a number of occasions without me knowing it! How do you like that! After 70 years of marriage, the truth finally comes out!

When I started working for Chick Webb, I introduced Beth to both Chick and Ella. Of course, over the years, Beth and Ella became friends. Knowing that Beth was indeed the right girl for me, I proposed to her and she accepted.

On September 22, 1938, Beth and I were married in a small ceremony with both our families in attendance. We were married at the Essex House on Central Park South in New York City. We sailed off into the sunset to Bermuda on our ten-day honeymoon.

Beth and I had a fabulous time in Bermuda and both of us got great tans. On the return sail home we got caught in the worst hurricane in a decade. When we disembarked the *Grace Line* in New York, we were green as cucumbers! The last few days on the ship was a bumpy ride that caused almost everyone on board to turn various shades of green!

Upon our return, the band played a couple of local gigs before going into the RCA-Victor studios in New York, on November 3, 1938, to cut our first sides on the Bluebird label. We were all excited.

We recorded six tunes that afternoon—three instrumentals: "Alexander's Swinging," my composition which we used as our theme song, and my arrangements of "On The Road To Mandalay" and Cole Porter's "Night and Day."

Also on this first recording session we recorded three vocals, including two charts of mine that were previously cut by Chick and Ella: "Gotta Pebble In My Shoe," a collaborative composition between Charlie Tobias and me which Chick recorded on August 17, 1938, and "I Found A Yellow Basket," which Chick recorded a month before our version.

Since "Gotta Pebble in My Shoe" was my song, it behooved me to record my own version of it. It's only natural for a composer to want to record his own works. Out of courtesy to Ella and because the following two songs hit the chart, I recorded my version of "I Found a Yellowbasket" and "F.D.R. Jones," which Ella had recorded in October. The vocalist on our versions was Jane Dover, who joined the band during the middle of November. Our first band vocalist, Shirley Brown, only stayed with us a few months.

While Jane was with us, she married Marty Melcher, who at that time was doing publicity for my band. (More about Marty later.) He later married Patty Andrews and Doris Day. Marty ended up marrying three girl singers. That was his thing, I guess.

Originally, I had used "Alexander's Ragtime Band" as my theme song, which was a natural for me. But when I started to play it on the air, I received a cease-and-desist telegram from Irving Berlin's publishing company stating that Mr. Berlin didn't want anyone associated with that song except himself. So I had to write another theme, which I called "Alexander's Swinging." I was never really happy with it, but it served its purpose for when I was on the air.

To be quite honest, I wasn't too happy with my band in the beginning. I especially wasn't happy with the rhythm section. I kept changing things, which I hated to do. Our drummer, Roger Segan, wasn't making it. He was great in a small group setting, but he didn't have the swing and the drive to really work effectively with a larger band, so I had to replace him. This real-life scenerio reminded me of a tongue-in-cheek story that was told about drummers who found themselves in a similar situation: There was this drummer who was playing in a band. He was the best friend of the band's leader. They had gone to school together. The drummer wasn't playing too well; he kept playing behind the beat all the time. The other members of the band were starting to complain saying that they couldn't play with this particular drummer, yet the leader was reluctant to fire him because of their close friendship. Finally, when push came to shove, the leader fired the drummer. The drummer was so dispondant that he went down to the railroad tracks and threw himself *behind* the train.

Looking back over my band's recorded material, we did a lot of covers of popular tunes such as "Digga-Digga Do," "Dancing in the Dark," "The Moon of Manakoora," "If I Didn't Care," "Way Down Yonder in New Orleans," "Thou Swell," "Six Lessons From Madame La

Zonga," "Cherry," and "The Jumpin' Jive." Overall, Eli Oberstein was very good to us. He gave us what I thought were good tunes to record. Of course, he was under pressure from song publishers, too, to record their things. However, in retrospect, I wish I'd been more assertive in having had a say in what my band recorded.

We were the first, however, to record "Let There Be Love," a popular song with music by Lionel Rand and lyrics by Ian Grant. We recorded it on May 25, 1939, with the flip-side tune of "In the Middle of a Dream." Our band vocalist at the time, Phyllis Kenny, who joined us in March, did a nice job on both tunes. "Let There Be Love" has become a well-known standard and was recorded by many artists at the time, including Kay Kyser, Jimmy Dorsey, The Andrews Sisters, Abe Lyman, Johnny McGee, Sammy Kaye and Al Donahue, among others.

Much to my disappointment, my recordings didn't sell that well. I credit much of that to not having a distictive sound as did some of my contemporaries. My band concentrated on an ensemble sound than it did showcasing individual soloists. We featured soloists, to be sure, but to do that consistently, we had to have outstanding jazz players. That's something I didn't have. Plus, I was in competition at the time with big-name fellow label mates: Glenn Miller, Artie Shaw, Tommy Dorsey, Benny Goodman, Bunny Berigan, Shep Fields, and even Larry Clinton.

During the first years of running my band, our favorite spot to play in New York City was the Roseland Ballroom on Broadway at 51st Street. It was our favorite spot because we played there for extended engagements (maybe three weeks at a time) and we were on the air at least three times a week. Roseland employed about a dozen or so ladies called "hostesses," for whom single male patrons could dance with after purchasing "dance tickets." Dance tickets were going for 11 cents a dance or $1.50 a half-hour while tuxedoed bouncers, politely known as "housemen," tried to oversee propriety. One of the strict rules of the management was that there could be no fraternizing with the hostesses. Now, there was one very pretty hostess, who winked or who would blow a kiss to me whenever she danced by. Being a young, 23-year-old, red-blooded man, I was naturally flattered. However, I was married just a short time so I kept my head about it and I didn't pursue the flirtation, much to her displeasure. She then started the same routine with Jerry Rosa, one of our trombone players in the band. Jerry made a date with her after the job and had a wonderful, wild evening. Two days later Jerry came down with a serious infection. In those days it was called "the clap" (gonorrhea). He got over it, but for years later every time I saw Jerry I would tell him I was in his debt and I thanked him profusely!

Another memorable Roseland Ballroom moment came in mid-1939 which played an important part in my career and personal friendship. A young man came over to me where I was resting between sets and said, "Mr. Alexander, my name is Sid Feller. I'm a trumpet player and arranger and I'd love to write an arrangement for your band."

This was a replay, or *deja vu*, of how I introduced myself to Chick Webb. So I said to Sid, "Sure, go ahead." I also explained to him that I couldn't afford to buy any more arrangements at the time, but he said he wanted to do it anyway.

A few days later he arrived at my rehearsal with his chart, "La Rosita." It was really very well written. We ended up recording it on the Bluebird label on June 21, 1939. Sid then joined Jack Teagarden's outfit for a short while before being drafted into the Army. While serving in the Army band, he continued to write and sent me arrangements even though I couldn't pay him very much. After his discharge, he toured for several years with Carmen Cavallero.

We then became good friends. Both our wives liked each other very much and we socialized very often. Sid and his wife, Gertrude, moved out to California in 1950, where he became one of the musical directors at Capitol Records. I included Sid in many of my musical projects. He helped me on a number of television film projects as well as helping me on some arrangements for Gordon MacRae and later when I was rushed on projects for *The Dean Martin Show*. Sid joined the staff of ABC-Paramount Records and, with Don Costa, greatly helped to build the label's success.

In 1960, Sid began a 25-year collaboration with singer Ray Charles following Charles' departure from Atlantic Records. Charles once said of him, "If they call me a genius, then Sid Feller is Einstein."

From 1969 to 1974, Sid worked as an arranger for *The Flip Wilson Show*. He also worked on numerous television specials. Sid passed away in February 2006, at age 89. He was a talented, good friend who played an important role in my life and times.

When my band went on the road, we did fairly well for a while even though we never really made any big money. We first got around by bus, and when we weren't doing so hot, we traveled in cars. Like most bands, we usually didn't take our wives with us when we were doing one-night stands. In the beginning, Beth traveled with the band and me until she became pregnant with our first daughter. She hated it when we ate at "greasy spoons." All she would eat at these places were things that were packaged, like crackers or small containers of milk. She wouldn't eat anything else. Shortly after that, she became pregnant with our first daughter, so she had to stay home.

MCA booked us at many of the ballrooms throughout the New England area that were either owned or controlled by the Shribman Brothers—Cy and Charlie. They were the big bookers of one-nighters through New England. They were very nice guys, very honest.

Cy Shribman, who was Glenn Miller's benefactor, did most of the front work for getting bands gigs at their dance spots. Whenever we played the Shribman Brothers' dates in New England, such as Boston's Roseland State Ballroom, we got paid off in two-dollar bills. Two-dollar bills were very big in the New England area for some reason or another. Half the money of what we contracted for was deposited in the bank before we got to the date, and the balance was paid in cash in two-dollar bills. We usually worked on a guarantee plus a percentage of the house. If we did well, we'd go over our guarantee. As far as I know, Cy always gave me an honest count.

The fact was, we weren't in any real competition with other bands and we took dates that maybe these other bands didn't want.

One date we were happy to get was during the 1939 New York World's Fair held in Flushing Meadows. The Fair was a huge tourist extravaganza that celebrated various cultures around the world as well as providing a glimpse of what lay ahead technologically for humanity. We were booked for a week at a venue at the Fair called "The Dancing Campus." A remote wire was provided for us and we broadcasted nightly from there. The Dancing Campus was a very popular site and it was located right behind Billy Rose's *Aquacade*. The show starred swimmer Eleanor Holm in what the Fair program called "a brilliant girl show of spectacular size and content." We had a great week playing for thousands of Fair-goers.

The summer of 1939 saw big changes in my life personally as well as professionally. In June, Chick Webb died. That was a devastating blow to me personally *and* professionally.

A few weeks later, on July 4, Butch Stone, music critic George S. Simon, and I were three out of over 60,000 fans sitting in Yankee Stadium bidding farewell to 36-year-old Lou Gehrig, the Bronx Bombers' slugger and Iron Horse First Baseman. Gehrig's uniform, No. 4, was retired that day, the first player ever have such an honor. There wasn't a dry eye in the place when Gehrig, who was dying of amyotrophic lateral sclerosis (ALS), gave his short farewell speech, in which he said, "I consider myself the luckiest man on the face of the earth." It was difficult to see one of my childhood athletic heroes go out the way Gehrig did. In recent years, fans voted this event as the fifth greatest moment in Major League Baseball history. I'm glad I was a part of it.

Major changes also occurred that summer concerning my band's recording career and with Eli Oberstein. It seems that William Berkson, Eli's attorney at RCA-Victor, was pocketing the Social Security monies that were deducted from our paychecks. He was discovered and was subsequently sent to jail. Eli was fired from RCA-Victor even though he had nothing to do with Berkson's illegal activities.

Not be be counted as down and out, Eli immediately formed United States Record Corporation, whose new label was Varsity Records the new company's blue 35-cent label. Varsity was to be a bargain re-issue label to remarket material from other labels such as Paramount, Gennett and Crown, while recording current artists. Eli felt that with his background and reputation that he could make a success out of anything, even forming a new independent record company. Eli asked me to come aboard on Varsity, which I did.

Other artists who signed on with Varsity included bandleaders Johnny Messner and Harry James, who stayed with Varsity for about a year beginning in January 1940 before re-signing to Columbia Records.

Eli thought it would be a good idea to give my band a "fresh" name, if you will, and so our records on Varsity were given the moniker of "Van Alexander and His Swingtime Band."

In August 1939, we cut our first six sides on the new Varsity label: "In The Mood," our cover of the Joe Garland tune that became a monster hit for Glenn Miller; "Honestly," "Scatterbrain," Many Dreams Ago," and "Angry," four pieces that featured our girl singer, Phyllis Kenny; and "Hot Dog Joe," my own novelty composition that featured Butch Stone on the vocal.

Phyllis Kenny stayed with me the longest as our girl singer, joining the band that February. She married Joel Livingston, our guitar player.

We also featured the romantic voice of our trombonist, Bill Schallenberger, on "Marie" and "I Wonder Who's Kissing Her Now?" (both were recorded in October 1939) and "Please Take a Letter, Miss Brown" (May 1940). Bill shortened his last name to Schallen before joining guitarist Alvino Rey in the summer of 1940. Bill and saxophonist

Skeets Herfurt later teamed up together on the vocal fun to help give
Alvino his first big hit in 1941 with "Deep in the Heart of Texas."

After leading the Fighting Coast Guard Band during World War II,
Bill later went on to be a much-in-demand studio musician at NBC in
New York, playing for a variety of radio and television shows, as well as
Broadway musicals. He died in November 2001, at age 84.

We also cut a pair of songs in April 1940 for Varsity—"The Woodpecker Song," and "I've Got My Eye on You"—that were pressed on the
Montgomery Ward Records label (Number 10039) as a promotional
gimmick for the department store chain. Both songs featured vocals by
Phyllis Kenny. It is my understanding that these Ward 78RPM platters
are quite rare and are considered to be collector's items.

I personally think we recorded better sides on Varisty than we had on
Bluebird. During our eight-month sojourn with Bluebird, we recorded 52
sides; and in the nine months we were with Varisty, we cut 30 sides.

I had an old friend named Morey Amsterdam, a comedian and master
of the one-liner, who performed in vaudeville and on radio before moving
to television, where he portrayed the wisecracking Buddy on *The Dick Van
Dyke Show*, in the 1960s. When I first met Morey, he was married to Mabel
Todd, an actress who played dumb blonde parts in quite a few pictures. In
1939, Morey and Mabel were signed by WOR Mutual Network in New
York City to do a weekly radio show called *The Laugh and Swing Club*. The
radio execs wanted the studio staff orchestra to provide the music, but Morey
insisted on using my band. We did the show for one season after which the
show was cancelled. During this time I got to meet some people who later
became famous. One of the comedy writers was Harry Crane, who went on
to write for many comedy shows. There was also a young, brash guy who
used to hang around the show who had been stricken with polio as a kid. His
name was Maurice Duke, who later managed Mickey Rooney. Guitarist
Tony Romano was also a featured performer on the show. He later traveled
with Bob Hope. Being on radio with Morey was a fun experience. Over the
years we kept in close contact until 1996, when Morey passed away at age 84.

In the early spring of 1940, drummer Irv Cottler joined my band,
coming over from Red Norvo's outfit. Irv was a fabulous timekeeper. He
later worked for Larry Clinton, Jimmy Dorsey and Les Brown before
being a first-call studio drummer in Los Angeles. For over 20 years, he
worked as Frank Sinatra's touring and recording session drummer. Frank
once called Irv, "The Best [Drummer] in the Business." Frank would get

no argument out of me on that point. Irv also worked for me on a few projects while at Capitol Records. I was honored to be Irv's Best Man at his wedding to Rose Mincielli. A month before he passed away, in August 1989, at age 71, Irv gave me an autograph picture of himself, which he inscribed, "To Van, You're still my best man." Irv was a dear friend and a helluva musician.

Another drummer of renown to filter through my band was Shelly Manne. He was 18 at the time and he did a couple of one-nighters with the band. My band was one of the first Big Bands he ever played with. He was great player at that time coupled with the fact that he was a gentleman who had a great sense of humor. He was a delight. Shelly went on to become an award-winning drummer in jazz circles and he was one of the early icons of the West Coast Jazz movement. He was always in high demand as a player. I was lucky to get him to play for my record dates when I signed on with Capitol Records years later. Shelly died much too young, at age 64, in 1984.

Other notable personnel who played in my band at various times included bassist Sandy Block; saxophonist Frank Socolow; trombonist Si Zentner ("Up A Lazy River" fame); and trumpeter Neal Hefti, who was a contributing architect to the compositional successes of Woody Herman's First Herd and Count Basie's band during the 1950s, and the composer of such jazz standards as "Li'l Darlin'," "Cute," and "Coral Reef." Neal also wrote background and theme music for television shows, including *Batman* and *The Odd Couple*, for which he received a handful of Grammy Award nominations and a Grammy for his work with the "Caped Crusader."

> *"I first met Van in 1942 or 1943 playing as a sideman in his band,"* recalled Neal Hefti, 86. *"I just left Nebraska and traveled straight to New York City to join the musicians' union, Local 802. As a transferee, union requirements dictated what kind of work and how much work we could do until we became a legal resident of that area. The waiting period was six months. During this six-month period, my ability to work in New York was limited by whatever the musicians' union would allow. One of the things I could do was to play incidental or substitute work. I could substitute a night here and there with any band. I got a call to join Van's band for a job in Van Courtland Park in the Upper Bronx. That's when I first met him.*

"I always thought of Van Alexander as one of the most well-dressed musicians-bandleaders. He looks like the epitome of the orchestra leaders of the 1940s playing at all the elegant places: the Glen Island Casino and the Avalon Ballroom on Catalina Island, places like that. He's a very elegant-looking man and he dresses that way.

"When I was getting more into arranging, I read Van's book. I was reading anything I could get my hands on about arranging.

"After I moved out to California in the mid-1960s, he and I were golfing buddies for a long, long time. He was fun to play with. He's probably in the Top Five of anybody's list of the Most Well-Liked Men in this town at least he is to me. I've never heard it any different from anybody else."

During the summer of 1940, Glenn Miller, who had one of the hottest bands in the land at that time, was playing at the Glen Island Casino in New Rochelle, New York, and we were playing a few miles from there at a place called Murray's at Tuckahoe. Beth and I rented a house in New Rochelle and two guys from Miller's band, Tex Beneke and Hal MacIntyre, rented a place right next door. We became friendly with them and their wives. On their night off, they came over to Murray's to hear our band and brought along their boss, Glenn Miller, with them. We were thrilled!

At the end of the evening, Glenn came up to me and introduced himself. He complimented me as to how the band sounded. He was very cordial. He liked my arrangement of "Two for Two." It was an unusual arrangement as it swung like mad. He thought it was "very inventive," he said. This was the one and only time Glenn and I ever crossed paths.

In the fall of 1940 we played a memorable three-week engagement at Loew's State Theater on Broadway in Times Square. We were part of a stage show with a number of acts in support of the movie *The Westerner*, starring Gary Cooper and Walter Brennan, which was being shown. I was being promoted in the theater ads as "King of the Swing Composers," while the band was introduced as providing "A New Style...A New Tempo...A New Swingsation."

Joining us on stage was Leroy "Slam" Stewart, the "Ace of the Bass." Slam was a versatile musician who was noted for his unusual solos by humming along as he bowed the strings of his bass. He later was an early player of bebop jazz and collaborated with guitarist Slim Gaillard to create some very successful "jive" music, of which "Flat Foot Floogie" became their most recognized hit.

Also on the bill at that Loew's Theater engagement was Allan Cross and Henry Dunn, "Radio's Song Stylists"; The Hartman's, "America's Outstanding Dance Satirists"; and the Three Trojans, "Collegiate Whirlwinds."

As a road band, we were doing all right—not great, but all right. We had been a unit now for two years and we were just about breaking even financially. We then received the wonderful news that we got booked for a possible three-week option at the famous Paramount Theater at Times Square. In the days of the motion picture-stage band combinations, the important factor in making a show a financial success for everyone concerned was the caliber of the picture. If you're lucky enough to do the date with a good picture, you could last at a theater for three or four weeks. When we got signed on at the Paramount Theater, we were hoping that we'd be teamed up with a blockbuster film.

We had a great stage show lined up, too. Joining us on the bill was violinist Matty Malneck and his band, and Cass Daley, who was a great comedian. We did five or six shows daily, starting at 11:00 in the morning.

However, as fate would have it, we didn't get that blockbuster movie for which we were hoping. Something happened at the last moment and the theater had to make a switch and we ended up getting a dud. That dud was *Geronimo,* an old-style Indian epic, starring Preston Foster, Ellen Drew, Andy Devine, and Gene Lockhart. To put it simply: it was a pretty bad movie. It didn't "take" with moviegoers. So, along with *Geronimo,* we had one fast week at the Paramount and we were out.

The Paramount Theater gig was the best price we ever had for a week's stay, too. If we had gotten another two- or three-week option, we would have gotten healthy.

We continued to limp along for a little while longer, but I saw the handwriting on the wall. Since we didn't have any hit records, I guess that the demand for my band wasn't there. Because of "A-Tisket, A-Tasket," Eli Oberstein thought I would produce a lot more hit songs. We were both disappointed on that point. I remember there were times when Joe Glaser, my manager, would have to make deals with MCA saying if a venue wanted Les Brown, they would also have to take Van Alexander. As time went on, the competition of the real Big Bands became stiffer.

We had a good band, but none of the musicians took it too seriously. We were all young. They were all good musicians, but not too dedicated. It was sort of a loose band and I wasn't a tyrant. Looking back, I could have been a lot stricter and more dedicated myself. By this time, to be honest, my heart was actually more into arranging than it was at being a bandleader. I was kept busy writing arrangements and keeping our library up. That's where my forté was.

After we recorded our final four sides in May 1940, Varsity Records also gave up the ghost. This also reminds me of an interesting story about Eli Oberstein: Eli had a thing going with his attractive secretary, but he was married to a stately-looking, dowager-type woman. Eli told his wife he had to go to the West Coast for business. His wife found out that Eli's secretary was tagging along and that both would be traveling to Los Angeles on the Super Chief. Thinking it best to be on the safe side, Eli and his girlfriend got off the train in nearby Pasadena. But as they got off, standing there tapping her foot and looking as stern as Margaret Dumont (from the Marx Brothers pictures) was Mrs. Oberstein. A nasty divorce followed.

After Varsity Records, Eli went on to own Rondo Records in the mid-1950s. He died on June 12, 1960, at age 60.

A few months after our time with Varsity Records ended, I disbanded my full-time touring band, but I still kept the band together to play whatever we could pick up—weekend things, individual dances, etc. I know Joe Glaser became a little disenchanted, not being able to sell the band as he wanted.

However, I was always a forward-looking person, so I started to teach privately, having about twenty pupils, including Johnny Mandel, who went on to earn Academy Award and Grammy Award accolades for his compositions and arrangements, and Ian Bernard, who became the arranger/conductor for television's *Rowan and Martin's Laugh-In* in the late 1960s. Teaching kept me busy for a while. I was also writing stock arrangements for the music publishers and writing outside arrangements for different bands. I was kept busy. I felt bad that I sort of "abandoned" some of the guys in my band who were depending on me, but there was nothing I could do about it.

The date June 23, 1941, was a milestone for Beth and me that forever changed our lives. It was on this day that Beth and I became the proud parents of a beautiful seven-pound baby girl. We named her Lynn. My pick-up band was playing at The Steel Pier in Atlantic City, New

Jersey, when Beth went into labor. I drove home just in time to be there when our precious angel was born. Now Beth would be content to stay home and take care of Lynn.

Six months later, a milestone that forever changed the lives of all Americans—and the world—took place half-a-world away on the small island of Oahu in the Hawaiian Islands. The place: Pearl Harbor. The date: December 7, 1941, a "date," President Franklin Roosevelt said, "which will live in infamy."

We had just played in a show at the War Memorial Auditorium in Buffalo, New York, and we were driving back home to New York in our cars when we heard the announcement on the car radio about the surprise attack on Pearl Harbor by the Japanese. I couldn't believe it. The first thing I said was, "Where in the hell is Pearl Harbor?" I think a lot of people probably asked that same question when they heard the news. Once reality set in, my immediate reaction was, "What nerve of those little bastards to do a terrible thing like that!"

With the United States now engaged in World War II, most of the good young musicians were being drafted. It was difficult getting quality players. We entertained the troops, playing at various military installations around the New York area. Sometimes we were paid off with gas-ration coupons, which we didn't mind as gas was being rationed as part of the war effort.

I was classified 1-A and I was fully expecting to get my draft notice any day. In the meantime, I continued working. We were able to record a pair of standard jazz songs—"Indiana Blues" and "Lonesome Me"—for Beacon Records, an independent label that was launched in 1942 by Joe Davis.

We then recorded "Margie," the title song for the soundtrack for a Soundie by the same name. Soundies were the prehistoric version to music videos. Soundies were three-to-five-minute black-and-white films that were designed to be seen on self-contained, coin-operated, 16mm rear-projection machines called Panoramas. They were located in nightclubs, bars, restaurants and other public places.

Doing a Soundie allowed listeners to put a face with the person creating the music. What we did in this short film was nothing to rave about, but it afforded greater exposure for the band and me. Such exposure would definitely be beneficial to us.

My band was featured in *Margie* along with Lew Hearn and Ann Mace. In my band at the time were Buddy Colaneri, Irv Friedman, Red

Schwartz, and Danny Wilson, trumpets; Mike Chen, and Buck Scott, trombones; Frank Socolow on tenor sax, plus three other saxophonists; Jimmy Norton, guitar; Louis Spinell, bass; Bobby Rickey, drums; me, piano; and Betty Carr was doing the vocal.

I continued to do outside work for other bands such as Larry Clinton, Les Brown, Kay Kyser, and for the wonderful black bands of Lucky Millinder, Cab Calloway and Les Hite. The musicians' union strike was in full swing at this time so my work with these bands wasn't documented on record.

Les Hite hired me to write about a dozen or so charts for his band as he really liked my arrangements. He was working at a place in New Jersey at the time. Les was a nice guy. His Big Band, known as Sebastian's Cotton Club Orchestra, primarily played in Los Angeles, though they occasionally went on tour. Les always had a very good, but unfortuantely, very underrated band. Musicians who played in various manifestations of his band include Lionel Hampton; saxophonist Marshall Royal, trombonists Lawrence Brown and Britt Woodman; guitarist/blues singer T-Bone Walker; and trumpeters Dizzy Gillespie and Joe Wilder.

> *"I first met Van when I was in Les Hite's band in early 1942, I just come out of high school,"* said Joe Wilder, 86. *"Van was a very nice guy, very friendly. War songs and pretty ballads were real popular at that time and that's what Van arranged for Les' band. They were pretty pieces that contrasted Les' style, and what Van wrote for the band really sounded great."*

Speaking of Lionel Hampton…Hamp came to my apartment once when I was still working for Chick Webb and together we wrote a tune while sitting at the piano. It was called "Jiving the Vibes." He recorded it on February 8, 1937. Hamp was still playing vibraharp with Benny Goodman at that time, and got some fellow band members from Benny's band to do a "pick-up" recording session. When the record was released, he never put my name as co-composer of the tune. I didn't know anything about copyrights at that time, so I never pursued any action.

On October 25, 1943, Beth and I celebrated another milestone in our lives: the birth of our second daughter, Joyce. Joyce's birth was announced in Walter Winchell's column in the *New York Daily News*.

Beth was having the time of her life with our two beautiful daughters—dressing them up and showing them off in Central Park. Isabelle Joseph, a wonderful lady we affectionately called "Bobo," helped Beth. Bobo was a great cook and baker. She had been employed by Beth's mother, Leah Baremore, when Beth and her sister, Carolyn, were small girls. Now, Bobo was working for us. We considered her a member of our family until she passed away in 1961.

My draft notice finally came in the mail and I was to report to a place in downtown Manhattan. Two days before I was ready to go, the order was rescinded as fathers over 28 years of age with children were exempted from active military service. In lieu of military service, I had to get a defense job.

I worked at a meatpacking plant in Lower Manhattan. I unpacked beef from the refrigerated rail cars for the Russian War Relief. The Russians were our allies at the time. I worked the 5 a.m.-to -11 a.m. shift.

I was also writing for Abe Lyman at the time. His band, The Californians, was playing at the Strand Theater. Abe got sick one day and he asked me to front his band for him. I was able to get off work a little early that day to make the first morning show which started at 11. At the theater I did a "quick change," taking off the old work clothes I had on and dressing into a tuxedo before going on stage. When I came home to our apartment on West End Avenue that evening, I had my work clothes on and the doorman said, "Excuse me, sir, you can't go in this way. The service entrance is around back." The doorman, thinking I was a janitor or maintenance man, didn't recognize me.

I worked at that meatpacking job until mid-1944. The war was winding down and the number of people for this kind of work wasn't needed.

My band did another successful stint at Loew's State Theater in the early spring of 1944. Sharing the stage with us was Mexican actor and singer Tito Guizar, and that great lady of song Mildred Bailey, noted for her many jazz vocals, including "Rockin' Chair." The movie that was playing was William Saroyan's *The Human Comedy* starring Mickey Rooney. Mickey, whose real name was Joe Yule, Jr., was nominated for an Academy Award for Best Actor in that film.

I then did some work for bandleader Tommy Tucker. He wanted to deviate from his "Mickey Mouse" sound which had gained him popularity with his 1941 hit, "I Don't Want to Set the World on Fire." Tommy now wanted to lead a swing band.

Joe Galkin, Tommy's manager, who was a rotund guy and lots of fun, got me the deal with Tommy. Beth and I traveled with Joe and his wife by car to Miami to meet Tommy and to talk over the particulars. I had a nice relationship with Tommy. I did about a dozen arrangements for him. Claude Hopkins and Fred Norman also wrote some things for his new band. The swing band idea didn't work out for Tommy and he eventually went back to his original sound.

My band then did a weekend gig for a month at the Allegheny Theater in North Philadelphia. What makes this engagement stand out in my mind was one of the acts on the bill was a young teenage comic by the name of Jerry Lewis, who was doing a Record Act, in which he mimed lyrics of operatic and popular songs to a phonograph while wearing funny hats. He was very funny. On the way home on the train, Jerry came up to me and asked me for my autograph.

During the late 1960s, I was working on a musical score at Columbia Studios, and Jerry, who was then producing pictures, had an office there.

I walked by his office one day and his door was open. I popped my head inside and said, "Hi, Jerry!"

He looked up and smiled and said, "Hey, Van! Come here. Remember when we played that theater in Philadelphia?"

"Yeah, I do," I said.

"Do you remember what was on the bill?"

"No, I sure don't, Jerry."

"There was Sharkey the Seal, a dance team..." He went through the line-up of that theater date.

I later found out that Jerry has a photographic memory and he remembers everybody's telephone number. Jerry was OK with me.

Toward the end of 1945, with the war over, the band business looked lean. I had been fortunate in keeping what I had going even on a part-time basis. My manager, Joe Glaser, then put together a deal for me that would later change my life.

Joe arranged a one-month engagement for my band and me to perform at the Capitol Theater in New York backing up Bob Crosby. Bob, the baby brother of crooner Bing Crosby, was a singer himself who, ten years earlier, led a truly swinging orchestra that featured the Dixieland music of his small group, The Bob Cats. Bob had just been released from the service after serving as an officer in the Navy. He led a touring military band that went island hopping in the Pacific, and he was ready to resume his civilian career as an entertainer.

During the war, the Capitol Theater was only showing movies with no stage band show and they now wanted to re-activate their band policy. Bob didn't have a band and I did, so Joe Glaser suggested that Bob use my band and have it billed as "Bob Crosby with the Van Alexander Orchestra."

Five years before I began my association with Bob Crosby, he put in a complimentary word about my band over his *Camel Caravan* radio show. Bob was broadcasting live from the Empire Theater in Syracuse, New York, on Saturday, April 6, 1940. He was doing some light-hearted bantering with Kurt Curtis, a junior from the university, who was telling Bob about Syracuse University's Junior Prom and its Hawaiian theme, which was held the night before at nearby Piney Hill. My band played for that Junior Prom. When Bob asked Kurt who played the sweet music for the prom, the young college student replied, "Van Alexander," to which Bob then said, "That's a real up-and-coming outfit."

We had a wonderful four weeks together at the Capitol Theater. Joan Edwards, the *Lucky Strike Hit Parade* girl, was also on the bill, as was the great dance team Mary Rae and Naldie.

Bob and I hit it off so well that at the end of that month-long gig, he asked me, "Have you ever thought of coming out to California? I'm going to relocate there to do radio and television. I'd like you to join me. You can put a band together for me and do all the arrangements."

I gave Bob's offer some serious thought. I saw the handwriting on the wall as far as the Big Bands were concerned. I thought it would be a good opportunity for me. Television was is its infancy and it would be a good chance for me to get my foot in the door. I talked it over with Beth, and she was for it. I then told Bob I was in.

And so a memorable chapter in my life was coming to an end and a bright, new chapter to be written 3,000 miles away in sunny California was just beginning.

CHAPTER SIX

CALIFORNIA, HERE I COME!

Affter I agreed to join Bob Crosby, Beth and I decided that we shouldn't just pull up stakes blindly to move out to California. The plan was that I would go out to the Golden State alone to check things out and once I felt that everything would be OK, then Beth and the girls would come join me.

In early November 1945, I boarded the Super Chief at Pennsylvania Station in New York and headed out to Los Angeles, at my own expense, by the way.

After I arrived in Los Angeles, I stayed for about six weeks with Uncle Henry, my father's brother, and his wife, Elsie, and their daughter, Ruth. They were very gracious and they treated me like royalty.

I immediately began putting together a band. Normally, there is a six-month waiting period for transferees before they can get union jobs in a new local. In this instance, knowing people in high places turned out to be a blessing for me. Joe Glaser, my now-former manager from New York, somehow pulled some strings for me in having the waiting period waived with the musicians' union here in Los Angeles. I still don't know even to this day how he did it, but I was admitted immediately as a member of Local 47. This gave me a free hand in securing the musicians I needed.

The band I put together was a wonderful sounding, tight-knit group comprised of many former Big Band stalwarts who migrated to Hollywood after the war to do studio and recording work.

In the beginning, trumpeter Billy May, an alumnus of the Charlie Barnet and Glenn Miller bands, was with us. Billy was already based in L.A. doing studio work at the time. Trumpeter Johnny Best, who played with Artie Shaw, Glenn Miller, Crosby, and Benny Goodman, was also in the band, as was guitarist Bob Bain, who later earned his place as the number one guitarist for many Hollywood studios and was a mainstay with the wonderful *Tonight Show* band. Clarinetist Matty Matlock and bassist Bob Haggart, both Bob Crosby alums, were also signed on. I also brought in a trumpet player friend of mine I knew from New York named Truman Quigley.

Bob kept me busy writing quite a few Dixieland things since he was so closely associated with that genre of music, as well as some ballads, as Bob was an amiable singer. Bob liked my work and how the band sounded. Things were coming together nicely and I felt secure enough in my job to have Beth and the girls, and Bobo make the move to join me.

Apartments were impossible to find as post-war housing was in high demand. So we rented a two-and-half-room suite at the famed eleven-story Knickerbocker Hotel on Ivar Avenue near Hollywood and Vine in Hollywood. It cost quite a stipend, but that's where the five of us lived for the next six weeks. In fact, the timing was just right as we were fortunate to have spent our first Christmas together in California. Beth and I even took the girls to see the popular "Santa Claus Lane Parade" along Hollywood Boulevard. The girls loved it! It was the first parade to resume after a three-year suspension due to the war.

After writing the initial arrangements, Bob then wanted me to travel with the band, which was not my understanding of our deal at all. I had enough of traveling with my own band, so I wasn't too keen on Bob's idea. I relented and I did a few road dates, but it was pretty rough.

One day my friend, Mickey Goldsen, another George Washington High School alumnus who headed Capitol Records' publishing division throughout the 1940s and who later went on to establish Criterion Music, an independent music-publishing firm in Los Angeles, asked me to do a band stock arrangement for him on the song, "Dream," which the Pied Pipers turned into a big hit. I welcomed the side job to earn a little extra income.

I drove to Mickey's office late the following evening to begin working on the arrangement when who walks in but dear ol' Bob. He was fit-to-be-tied.

"What the hell are you doing, Van?" he yelled at me. "I'm paying you good money to write for *me*."

"I do write arrangements for you, Bob," I shot back. "But if I want to stay up all night on my own time to write something for a friend, I should be able to do it."

That didn't sit well with Bob, and he immediately turned on his heels and stormed out of the room.

Our relationship over the next week wasn't as cordial as it was in the past. Bob didn't have too much to say to me and what he did have to say was just business related—short and to the point.

Not long afterwards, we did a date in Sacramento. It went well and after the gig Bob asked me to drive his wife, June, back to Los Angeles. I agreed.

June and I were having a pleasant drive back when she said to me, "Aren't you glad you are out here in California, away from all the Jews in New York?"

"I beg your pardon?" I replied.

"You know, those elements in New York are terrible," she said.

"Well, June, evidentially you didn't realize that I'm Jewish," I said.

Caught off guard, June became very apologetic, saying that she didn't mean to offend me. She then came up with the typical and usual response that some of her dearest friends are Jewish.

"Oh, Gil Rodin is Jewish, and he's the godfather to our son..."

It was a very sticky moment. I'm sure what was said must have been relayed back to Bob. A few weeks later I received a surprise call from MCA telling me that Bob wasn't happy with what I was doing and that he wanted to make a change.

"Well, what about my contract?" I asked the MCA person.

"I'm not certain if your contract will hold up," the MCA said.

"It will through the musicians' union," I shot back.

I brought a lawsuit against Bob through the musicians' union for breach of contract. Judgment was deferred to me and Bob had to pay me a year's salary. So after three short months working for Bob, I was out of a job. Thank goodness for Joe Glaser's intervention for me in getting me in with the union so quickly. At this point in time, I would still have had three more months to go in my waiting period with the union and my case against Bob would have ultimately been dismissed.

Shortly after my departure, Bob landed his own daily fifteen-minute radio musical variety show called *Club 15*. It ran from 1946 through 1952. This added salt to my wound, as this could have been my gig. Bob ended up hiring Jerry Gray as his arranger-conductor. Jerry, who was a brilliant arranger, worked for Artie Shaw and Glenn Miller (in both his civilian and military outfits) before going on to lead his own band in the 1950s.

Bob had a tremendous ego and all he ever tried to do was to cash in on his brother Bing's popularity. I used to tell a joke that the last time I saw Bob Crosby he was walking down Lover's Lane holding his own hand. I can laugh about all this now, but at the time it was disastrous.

I am happy to say that Bob and I patched up our differences years before he passed away of cancer in 1993.

While I was working for Bob and thinking that my job with him was secure, I went out on a limb to put a down payment on our first home. Taking refuge in the Knickerbocker Hotel was a temporary housing solution for my family and me, and after six weeks there, it was time to find a permanent place where we could lay some roots.

With some financial help from my parents and Uncle Henry, and borrowing the limit on my life insurance policy, we bought a beautiful Spanish-style home on Crest Drive in West Los Angeles. It had a beautiful bricked backyard with orange trees and a wonderful playhouse in the back that soon became the girls' dollhouse.

Not long after we moved in, Beth's parents, Barry and Leah Baremore, along with Leah's sister, Anna, also migrated to Los Angeles. Soon after that, Beth's sister, Carol, and her husband, Alfred, also made the move. They all took apartments close by on Shenandoah Street. I must admit it was nice to have the whole family together—good for Beth and good for the girls.

I was out in the cold, so to speak, after the Crosby affair and all sorts of worry went through my mind. I was 3,000 miles away from familiar territory. I had a little reputation back East, but no one knew me out here. It was then I found out that Hollywood was the only city in the world where a guy could die from encouragement! The year's salary that I won in the case against Bob helped a little, but I needed more income, so I looked for whatever work I could find.

What was a disaster at the time actually turned out to be a blessing in disguise. I probably wouldn't have gotten out to California if it weren't for dear ol' Bob.

Luckily, I had a few friends here in Los Angeles. One was Mickey Goldsen and the other was Howie Richmond, who was also a music publisher. Howie used to do publicity for my band back in New York. In 1949, he became one of the most successful music publishers around when he founded TRO Music, his independent music company. Along with Johnny Mercer and Abe Olman, a TRO Music senior partner, Howie helped create the Songwriters' Hall of Fame in 1969. Sixty years later, Howie's TRO Music is still going strong, as is Mickey's Criterion Music.

Both Mickey and Howie continued to give me work to do for their publishing firms, for which I shall always be in their debt.

Over the years I had gained a lot of experience, and, I would like to think, some wisdom at the art of arranging. Some of what I learned came from formal settings such as classes and in private tutorial lessons from a number of learned and talent individuals. But most of it was hands-on experience; learning by doing, and learning not only from my successes but also from my near-successes.

When I was teaching privately back in New York, many of my students lamented that there was no "textbook" as such to help guide them in their study of this craft. It was true. There was no popular book out on the market dealing with the "how-tos" of arranging.

During that time I began writing material in the hopes of one day having a book published on the subject. Along with my teaching, writing this book was a natural progression. Through the help of my friend Mickey Goldsen, I had such a book published in 1946 through his Criterion Music Corporation. I called the book *First Arrangement.* The book was geared for novice arrangers by giving them the fundamentals of orchestration along with information about each instrument with its ranges and capabilities. It was designed to help them write their "first arrangement."

The book did very well and to this day I have well-known people coming to me saying that they've used my book. It's very gratifying to hear. Some luminaries who have used *First Arrangement* include Quincy Jones, Elmer Bernstein, and Jonathan Tunick.

In 1995, when the American Society of Music Arrangers and Composers (ASMAC) were honoring Billy May and me, Quincy Jones wrote a letter of congratulations to both of us. In that letter he wrote, "In my teens, I must have worn out at least four copies of Van's book on arranging, reading them far into the night for many years."

In 2006, Jonathan Tunick, who was the musical arranger for the 2007 film, *Sweeney Todd: The Demon Barber of Fleet Street,* starring Johnny Depp, in a letter, wrote me: "I...thank you for having been my first teacher, both through *First Arrangement,* and subsequently the study and repeated playing of your many stock arrangements, which were agreed by all to be the very best of that genre. I decided at age twelve...that I wanted to start a band. With a copy of your book in hand, I sat down to create a library. I carefully followed your instructions and to my amazement what emerged actually sounded more or less like music...I'm glad to have the chance to thank you for starting me, without knowing it, on a path to an exciting and most satisfying life."

Wow! Reading such kudos makes it all worthwhile.

My book was updated in the 1960s and was retitled *First Chart*, to give it a more contemporary title. Musicians were to calling their written musical scores "charts" instead of "arrangements."

Then came my first break. Somewhere along the line, crooner Dennis Day heard about me and called me. He was looking for an arranger/conductor for his weekly song segment on *The Jack Benny Show*. He wasn't happy with the show's regular conductor, Mahlon Merrick. Dennis asked me to do an arrangement for him. I wasn't working at the time and I was happy to do it. He liked what I did and I was hired. Every week when Jack Benny would say over the radio, "Oh, sing Dennis!" Mahlon would step aside and I would step up in front of the band to conduct my arrangement for Dennis. It was a little embarrassing, but I was living by the old motto, "Friend or foe, get the dough." The motto continues to work for me today. I worked for Dennis Day for over a year and it got me started out here in L.A. Dennis died in 1988 of Lou Gehrig's disease (ALS).

Sometime during this period Cy Devore, who dressed a lot of celebrities at his very pricey clothing store on Vine Street in Hollywood, asked me to put together an eight-piece band to play for shows and for dancing at a nightclub called Slapsy Maxie's located on Wilshire Boulevard along the "Miracle Mile." Former boxing champ Max Rosenbloom owned the nightspot, but Cy held an interest in it.

It was to be a six-week gig and I saw the job as a gift from heaven. The first show consisted of Tony Canzoneri, the ex-welterweight boxing champ who was one of the few puglists to have won titles in three or more divisions; a dancer named Marc Platt; and an up-and-coming comic named Joey Adams. I also hired a great girl singer named Bunny Bishop who years later recorded with me for the Gordon MacRae-Dorothy Kirsten operetta *Kismet*. It was an enjoyable six weeks.

Shortly after the Slapsy Maxie engagement, Hershey Martin, an MCA agent, approached me. MCA was booking Lorraine Allen Cugat (the third of five wives of Latin bandleader Xavier Cugat) into the Last Frontier Hotel in Las Vegas. Hershey asked me to be her musical director for the engagement. I wrote a few arrangements for her, put a 12-piece band together, and went to Las Vegas for a month to direct the show. I took the job as I would have taken anything to make a few bucks at that time. One of the sax players in the band was Jay Cooper, who would become a famous music industry attorney. He was working his way through law school at the time.

We did the Last Frontier gig during the summer. Lynn and Joyce were on vacation from school, so Beth and the girls spent the month with me in hot Las Vegas. We had a good time.

Lorraine was a beautiful gal, but not a great singer. She had the name and the Las Frontier did some business because of her. I saw Lorraine again years later. She was at the Coconut Grove dancing with my old friend, Jonie Taps, from Columbia Pictures. (More about him later.)

I then received a call from Bob Stern, a publicity agent here in Los Angeles, inviting me to hear a two-sister singing act from Waco, Texas, calling themselves The Ewing Sisters. I listened to them and they were good. Jeanne and Jolaine Ewing had no formal musical training but they possessed a natural talent with a tight harmonic sound. They were very dear girls and I became very fond of them.

In the early fall of 1946, Stern asked me to arrange some tunes and to put together a trio so the Ewing Sisters could wax thirty transcription recordings for Standard Transcriptions to be played over the radio in order to help promote their career. Bassist Gene Englund and guitarist Tony Rizzi, with myself at the piano, played for the recording date.

The girls were gaining a little reputation in L.A. KTLA television took an interest in them and gave them a 15-minute musical show twice a week sponsored by the Curry Ice Cream Company. Gene Englund, Tony Rizzi and I were the musical accompaniment on the show, which lasted about four months.

Jeanne and Jolaine then did a few recordings on Capitol Records during the summer of 1951, with pianist Joe "Fingers" Carr, the stage name for Lou Busch, accompanied by my band. After which the girls got a three-week booking through MCA to play at the Flamingo Hotel in Las Vegas. During the Flamingo gig, Jeanne fell in love with some guy and got married soon after, which broke up the act. Jeanne has since passed away and Jolaine now lives in Maricopa, California.

I had been in California now for almost a year-and-a-half, and I was slowly making it. I was appreciative for the help I received along the way from friends in the music business and I was gradually beginning to make a name for myself in Los Angeles.

In the spring of 1947, I received a call from Irving Mills to write three original instrumental jazz arrangements that he wanted to record for his own record label called American Recording Artists (ARA). I jumped at the opportunity because I needed a job and some income.

Irving Mills was noted as a very shrewd but important music publisher, but he was also a Big Band promoter and was the guiding force behind Duke Ellington. The music industry often frowned on his ability to get his name included as lyricist on many of Duke's songs, such as "Solitude," "Sophisticated Lady," and "Mood Indigo."

Irving and I knew each other from New York and he was a pretty good friend of mine. One day, he invited another friend, Lud Gluskin, and me over to his place for cocktails. Lud was a bandleader who was quite successful leading his band all over Europe from the mid-1920s to the mid-1930s. The rise of Adolf Hitler made it difficult for Lud to find work in Central Europe, and he eventually decided to leave the Continent. Upon returning to the United States, Lud led dance bands and worked on radio. He took the position of director of music for CBS in 1937, working out of Hollywood.

After a few drinks I said to Irving, "Please tell me how you justify putting your name on Duke's 'It Don't Mean a Thing (If It Ain't Got That Swing).'"

He took one beat and said, "I gave Duke the title."

That was the end of that conversation.

Irving wanted each selection for my upcoming recording session to have the words "Blue Rhythm" in the song titles, as it was reflective of the name of one of the musical groups he led in the early days—"The Mills Blue Rhythm Band."

My compositions were entitled "Blue Rhythm Jam," "Blue Rhythm Blues," and "Blue Rhythm Bop." We recorded them on May 20, 1947, and I was given leadership credit on the label as "Van Alexander's Blue Rhythm Band."

The musicians on this recording date truly comprised an all-star band. On trumpets were Frank Beach, Chuck Peterson, and Charlie Shavers. On trombones we had Sid Harris, Si Zentner, and Charles Maxon. Eddie Rosa, Clint Neagley, Lucky Thompson, Stan Getz, and Butch Stone rounded out the saxophone section. Jimmy Rowles played piano; Tony Rizzi was on guitar. Arnold Fishkind was our bassist; and Don Lamond, who just came off the road with Woody Herman, was our drummer.

Tenor saxophonist Stan Getz was just a 20-year-old kid on these sessions with me. He already made his mark with Stan Kenton, Jimmy Dorsey and Benny Goodman. Soon after these recordings were made for me, Stan went on to join Woody Herman's Second Herd, or what is commonly referred to as "The Four Brothers Band." For over the next 40 years Stan stood tall as a giant in the jazz world until his death of liver cancer in 1991.

Five months later, on November 15, another manifestation of my Blue Rhythm Band was back in the studios once again to record two more of my original compositions on ARA Records using the same format as before. For this session we cut "Blue Rhythm Ramble" and "Blue Rhythm Bounce." The band personnel changed a bit from the first session, but we still had a line-up of heavy all-star hitters with Ray Linn and Jimmy Zito on trumpets; Juan Tizol on valve trombone; Eddie Rosa and the great Willie Smith on alto saxes; Herbie Haymer on tenor sax; and Butch Stone on baritone sax. The rhythm section included Wally Weschler on piano; Barney Kessel on guitar; Arnold Fishkind, bass; Irv Cottler, drums; and Charles Garble on vibes.

I was thrilled with meeting all the big name players and my things turned out great. However, when the records came out along with sheet music copies of my tunes, under each title was printed "Composed by Van Alexander and Irving Mills." Well, I wasn't in a position to ask any questions about Irving's sudden compositional "collaboration" with me as I needed the job and was reluctant to open a can of worms. But that was Irving Mills... He built an empire and died in 1985 a multi-millionaire.

In between the Irving Mills dates, I also led recording sessions on various independent labels for singers Jerry Wayne, Jerry Duane, Kay Brown, and Tommy Turner, and master harmonica player Leo Diamond.

With the new year of 1948, came another musicians' union strike call by American Federation of Musicians' president James Caesar Petrillo. This was the second musicians' union strike in six years. This meant that once again, no musician could enter a studio to record music. The strike was called in order to pressure record companies to make a better arrangement for paying royalties to recording artists. This strike lasted until mid-November.

The strike was a pain as Petrillo himself was at times. I was just starting to become well known in L.A. and I was being asked to do more and more record dates. So this near-year-long strike slowed things down for me a bit.

In early 1949, I arranged a couple of tunes and put a band together to accompany The Lancers, a popular male singing quartet that often did back-up vocals for Kay Starr, for a recording session for London Records. I also worked with The Lancers again for some recordings on Trend Records, an independent jazz label founded by Albert Marx. In late 1953, we recorded what would be a semi-hit record of the Jarrett Meacham tune called "Sweet Mama Tree Top Tall." It was a folk/gospel-tinged piece that stayed in the Top 40 for five weeks, peaking at number 13. The song was first recorded in the mid-1920s by the Birmingham Jubilee Singers and later by country singer Johnny Bond in the 1940s.

One of the most rewarding professional associations I ever had in my life was when I worked for Capitol Records. Capitol Records was the brainchild of composer Johnny Mercer. He wanted to form a West Coast recording company that would be "new" and innovative. He and partners, Buddy DeSylva and music store owner Glenn Wallichs, formed Capitol Records in 1942. From the get-go they produced hit after hit, until Capitol Records had quickly become one of the Big Four major record labels in the country behind RCA-Victor, Decca, and Columbia.

I came to Capitol through the benevolent friendship of Mickey Goldsen's secretary, Mildred Cavanaugh. Mildred was married to saxophonist/arranger Dave Cavanaugh., who was one of the first A&R (Artist & Repertoire) men at Capitol. Dave was a good friend of Mickey's because his wife worked for him. Dave helped to get my foot in the door at Capitol. I signed a non-exclusive contract with Capitol, which meant that I could work for other record labels if I wanted. Capitol would hire me for specific recording projects.

Artists on the Capitol Records roster at that time included Kay Starr, Louis Prima and Keely Smith, Les Paul and Mary Ford, "Tennessee" Ernie Ford, Mel Blanc, Ray Anthony, Nat "King" Cole, Margaret Whiting, Les Baxter, Nelson Riddle, Billy May, Ella Mae Morse, Stan Kenton, June Christy, Peggy Lee, Gisele MacKenzie, Stan Freberg, Dean Martin, Yogi Yorgesson, Tex Ritter, and Molly Bee, among others.

One of the first things I did on Capitol was to record a couple of novelty tunes with Butch Stone in March 1949: "Etiquette Blues" and "My Feet's Too Big." Butch was a star member of Les Brown's Band of Renown. Les relocated in Los Angeles a few years earlier as the musicial director for Bob Hope's radio show and tours. So it was great to have Butch in the same "neighborhood," so to speak, with me again.

When I started working for Capitol, Johnny Mercer was pretty much out of the picture as the hands-on founder of his recording company. He was spending most of his time composing. His other Capitol partners, Buddy DeSylva and Glenn Wallichs, were around, of course. I worked with other Capitol execs such as Dave Dexter as well as with other Capitol A&R men, including Voyle Gilmore, who produced a number of Frank Sinatra albums later on; Tom Morgan, who produced my *Home Of Happy Feet* album; Lee Gillette; and Ken Nelson, the Country-Western music A&R man.

The Capitol studios, in my mind, were the best. Everything about it, from their engineers to their echo chambers, was first-rate. Capitol was able to reproduce beautifully what we, as composers and arrangers, wrote. When I first started working at Capitol, their studios were located on Melrose Avenue in Hollywood. The current thirteen-story Capitol Records Towers, now a landmark site located on Vine Street near Hollywood Boulevard with its wonderful state-of-the-art recording studios, was built in 1956.

Capitol started me off working in its Western Music Department working with such artists as Tex Ritter and Molly Bee. I thought it was rather ironic that Capitol should get a city boy who was born and raised in Harlem to write Western music.

Molly Bee, a native of Beltbuckle, Tennessee, was only 13 when she signed with Capitol Records, releasing her first single, "Tennessee Tango." In November 1952, I worked with her on her first hit, "I Saw Mommy Kissing Santa Claus," rivaling Jimmy Boyd's version on Columbia Records for the top position. I worked with her on a number of different singles after that as her fan base grew. Molly was also a regular on *The Pinky Lee Show* and later on Tennessee Ernie Ford's daytime television show. By the end of the decade, Molly was so popular that her live shows were drawing large, record-breaking crowds.

Molly was a sweetheart to work with and the last I heard, she recorded an album a few years back and is still performing.

Singing cowboy star Maurice "Tex" Ritter's personality was as big and warm as his native Texas. A hero on the silver screen since the early 1930s, Tex was the first Western singer to sign on with Capitol when it started in 1942. His big, deep, lived-in voice brought a unique authenticity to the Western songs that he sang, more than any other singer of that genre of music, I suppose.

I worked with Tex on a number of singles and he was a delight. A pair of singles we recorded from 1954—"The Bandit" and "Prairie Home"— made their way onto a compilation album that was released four years later and that sold pretty well called *Tex Ritter: Songs from the Western Screen*. I also worked with Tex on a two-song children's album called *Tex Ritter Sings* that featured the songs "Muskrat" and "One Misty, Moisty Morning."

A number of years after Tex passed away in 1974, I was at a cocktail party that was also attended by Tex's son, John Ritter, who starred in the TV sitcoms *Three's Company* and *Hooperman*. I had never met John before, so I introduced myself to him. I told him that I worked with his father on a number of recordings while at Capitol Records. John was so excited and enthusiastic that he brought me around with him to every person at the party and told them about my involvement with his dad.

One of the truly consummate and versatile artists I had the pleasure to work with at Capitol was the fabulous Kay Starr. Kay can sing jazz, country, blues, and pop all equally well. Kay cut her teeth singing as a girl singer in the bands of Joe Venuti, Glenn Miller, Bob Crosby, and Charlie Barnet, before signing on with Capitol in 1945.

In 1952, she had a smash hit with "Wheel of Fortune," which stayed at number one on the charts for ten weeks, thus earning her a gold record. Other hits soon followed. Three years later, in 1955, Kay signed on with RCA-Victor, which produced "Rock and Roll Waltz," her second gold record and one of the biggest hits of 1956.

In 1959, Kay returned to Capitol. I arranged and conducted the material for *Movin'*, the first of four consecutive albums she recorded for Capitol after her three-year hiatus at RCA-Victor. During that summer, we recorded *Movin'*, which featured a number of standards such as "Indiana," "On a Slow Bloat to China," "Lazy River," and "Goin' to Chicago Blues," all done with a jazzy-bluesy feel to them.

The following year, Kay and I collaborated on the balance of our recording projects together with *Losers, Weepers*, *Movin' On Broadway*, and *Jazz Singer*. The latter album, recorded on June 11 and 18, featured "Hard-Hearted Hannah," an old gutbucket saloon song that Kay also sang in her live shows, much to her audiences' delight.

"Van is an elegant gentleman and he's proven himself as far as music is concerned," says Kay Starr, 86. "He taught me a lot of delicate things because I'm just an Oklahoma girl. If

anyone has the liking to any of those four albums I worked on with Van, I give the credit to him because he helped me to have a feeling for all kinds of music, more than what I had. He's really 'The Gentleman of Music.'"

Kay and I remain good friends to this day.

Truly the most "playful" assignments I had at Capitol during the mid-1950s was arranging the music and conducting the orchestra for a number of children's albums with voice actor and funnyman Mel Blanc. Known as the "Man of a Thousand Voices," Mel was a creative genius recognized for his work at Warner Bros. as the voice of such iconic characters as Bugs Bunny, Daffy Duck, Porky Pig, Sylvester the Cat, Tweety Bird, Foghorn Leghorn, Yosemite Sam, Speedy Gonzalez and Pepé LePew, and hundreds of others. In addition, Mel did the voice of cartoon character Woody Woodpecker as well as Barney Rubble on *The Flintstones* televison cartoon series. He was also a mainstay on both Jack Benny's radio and television programs.

Most of Mel's body of work doing children's albums were with Billy May, but some of the albums Mel and I did together in the early 1950s include *Bugs Bunny and Rabbit Seasoning, Daffy Duck's Feathered Friend, Daffy Duck's Duck Inn, Pied Piper Cat, Mel Blanc Sings Tweet and Toot and E.I.O. Songs, Woody Woodpecker and the Lost Monkey, Woody Woodpecker Meets Davey Crocket,* and *Happy Hippety Hopper,* about an adventurous but loveable Australian kangaroo.

Mel and I also recorded a handful of singles together. One funny single that stands out was "Yah, Das Ist Ein Christmas Tree," a Dave Cavanaugh and Sid Robin ditty recorded in March 1953, in which Mel sang in the character of a zany German holiday enthusiast in "schnitzelbank" fashion along with a host of other off-the-wall voice characterizations.

Anytime I'd do a project with Mel, I'd always have to make sure we'd limit the number of songs per session because Mel would invariably crack everyone up with his voice characterizations, and we'd end up having to do a number of retakes. It was all in good fun, of course, and Mel was a sweet guy. One just never knew what Mel would say and in what "character" he would say it. The animation world lost its most gifted voice when Mel died of a heart attack in 1989, at age 81.

Speaking more of children's albums...I also had the wonderful opportunity of working with entertainer Eddie Cantor on *Maxie the Taxi,* the story of a taxi driver who inadvertently picks up a bear as his fare at the zoo, logging their misadventures together.

Keely Smith was another consumate artist with whom I was privledged to work at Capitol. Long associated as the "straight act" with her husband, trumpeter Louis Prima, Keely and Louis were the undisputed "King and Queen of Las Vegas" throughout the 1950s, and have been credited with inventing the modern lounge act.

During the mid-1950s, Keely signed on to a solo recording career while still working with Louis. Her 1957 recording of "I Wish You Love," on the album by the same name, became such an enormous hit for Keely that it became her signature song. The following year Louis and Keely recorded "That Old Black Magic," which earned for them a Grammy Award.

It was around this period that I recorded a handful of singles with her at Capitol.

In recent years, Keely has experienced a resurgence of popularity with the retro-swing movement, using "Jump, Jive, and Wail" that she and Louis had made famous, as its anthem. She also recorded some critically acclaimed albums for Concord Records, including *Swing, Swing, Swing* (2000) and *Keely Sings Sinatra* (2001), for which she was nominated for a Grammy Award. On February 10, 2008, Keely performed "That Old Black Magic" with Kid Rock at the 50th Grammy Awards on CBS.

> *"Van is one of the best arrangers that I've ever known,"* said Keely Smith, 76. *"He's a gentleman and he worked well with the musicians. He knew how to handle the musicians. He was very easy to work with and he always made me feel very comfortable."*

Other Capitol artists with whom I recorded include bandleader Glen Gray and his Casa Loma Band; trumpeter Joe Graves and the Diggers; Dakota Staton; George Chakiris; Vonnie Taylor; and crooner Gordon MacRae (more about Gordon in the next chapter).

Throughout the 1950s I also recorded on MGM Records with Country singer Curly Wiggins and crooner Art Lund, who was Benny Goodman's boy vocalist a decade earlier. I also did work with the Jud Conlon Rhythmaries; Charlie Cal; singer Lorry Raine; Andy Williams; Norman Brooks, an Al Jolson sound-alike, on Verve Records; veteran jazz and blues vocalist Mavis Rivers on Reprise Records; Anna Maria Alberghetti; and the vocal trio of Jane Russell, Connie Haines and Beryl Davis.

In 1953, I teamed up with Doris Day to cut a dozen transcription recordings of standard songs, including "I Can't Give You Anything But Love," "A Hundred Years From Today," "Blue Skies," "My Blue Heaven," "Coffee, Cigarettes and Memories," and "Sentimental Journey," a reprise of the blockbuster hit she sang eight years earlier as a band singer with Les Brown. We even did "I've Gotta Sing Away These Blues," which we re-recorded commercially for Columbia in December 1955. On the flip side of that record was "Que Sera, Sera," which she did with Frank DeVol, and, subsequently, it became her biggest hit as well as her theme song.

One of the biggest thrills for me personally and professionally, was to work on two albums at Capitol with the great trombonist Jack Teagarden. When it comes to playing the slide trombone and singing the blues, no one can match "Big T." In January 1956, I was able to collect a fantastic assortment of all-star musicians for the session. The wonderful Eddie Miller played tenor sax. Nick Fatool was on drums. Manny Klein and Jack's younger brother, Charlie Teagarden, played trumpets. Ray Sherman was on piano, and Si Zentner was on trombone; and Willie Schwartz and Gus Bivona, played alto saxes and clarinets. The result was *This Is Teagarden*, and the project, I'm proud to say, is pure Jackson T all the way. The following year we did a follow-up album, *Swing Low, Sweet Spiritual*, which, I think, turned out to be another fine project.

I was then presented with the opportunity of creating my own musical gems when Capitol Records offered me an exclusive contract to record three albums for them under my own name. It was 1958, and the Savoy Ballroom had closed its doors for good. Dave Cavanaugh came up with an idea to do a record to salute some of the great bands and tunes that had been featured there.

"With your past association with the Savoy Ballroom, Van, why don't you do an album recalling as to what things sounded like there, and do it with a studio band," Dave said to me.

"That sounds like a fabulous idea, Dave," I replied. "I have very fond memories of the Savoy. Let's do it!"

I immediately went to work picking out the material and writing updated arrangements. The album contained recreations of songs associated with many of the black bands that had left their mark at the Savoy. But, in many cases, the recreations were so much better than the originals. We did Andy Kirk's theme song, "Until the Real Thing Comes Along"; Lucky Millinder's "Ride, Red, Ride," which featured a vocal by trombonist Joe Howard and some great trumpet work by Shorty Sherock; Don Redman's "Chant Of The Weed"; Teddy Hill's "Uptown Rhapsody"; Fletcher Henderson's "Christopher Columbus"; Duke's "East St. Louis Toodle-Oo"; and Chick Webb's theme, "Let's Get Together," as well as "Stompin' at the Savoy" and "A-Tisket, A-Tasket."

"A-Tisket, A-Tasket" is the same arrangement that Ella sang, except on this recording we had eight brass and five saxes in the band, and we had stereo and reverb, and it sounded so much more alive than the original thing. But, Ella's record is still being played, and I'm just grateful and lucky that I found the time to do it, because Edgar Sampson could have done it.

Remaining band personnel included an all-star line up with Conrad Gozzo, Manny Klein, and Uan Rasey, trumpets; Ed Kusby, Tommy Pederson, and Ken Shroyer, trombones; Paul Horn, Jules Jacob, Plas Johnson, Abe Most and Butch Stone, saxophones; Paul Smith, piano; Barney Kessel, guitar; Joe Mondragon, bass; and Shelly Manne and Irv Cottler on drums.

The album was originally called *The Home of Happy Feet*, the pseudo-name for the Savoy Ballroom. However, nobody knew what "the home of happy feet" was, so Capitol withdrew the album and reissued it in May 1960 under a different name, calling it *The Savoy Stomp*. Consequently, the "new" album sold like hot cakes, but I wish they had sold like records!

My second album, *Let's Dance the Last Dance*, recorded in October 1960, was an album of "mood music," so to speak, reflective of pretty tunes that would be played at the final dance of the evening, such as "I'll Be Seeing You," "Autumn Leaves," "I'll See You in My Dreams," Goodnight Sweetheart," and "Melancholy Serenade," the theme song of *The Honeymooners'* television show, starring Jackie Gleason, Audrey Meadows and Art Carney.

My final album, *Swing! Staged for Sound*, recorded in December 1961, was a series of duets accompanied by a Big Band. I used guitarist Bob Bain for this session. We had three drummers—Shelly Manne, Milt Holland and Irv Cottler, and two trombones—Milt Bernhart and Dick Kenney. Plas Johnson and Babe Russin were on tenor saxophones. Henri Rose and Bobby Stevenson were featured on two pianos on "I Won't Dance," an interpolation of Chopin's "Revolutionary Etude" that was tied into the final arrangement. It was a good album.

Capitol also employed three fabulous arrangers that were really superstars in their craft: Paul Weston, Billy May and Frank DeVol. I had known the names of these three gentlemen long before I met them.

Paul Weston started his career with Tommy Dorsey and later married singer Jo Stafford. When Capitol Records got off and running in 1942, Paul was the label's main arranger and orchestra leader. Paul was a deeply religious man and a great musical mind.

Billy May was synonymous with a slew of successful recording projects at Capitol, most noteworthy are his sessions with Frank Sinatra in the mid-to late 1950s.

Frank DeVol got his start as a saxophonist/arranger with Alvino Rey. Frank went on to marry singer Helen O'Connell while doing some acting in television.

When I started to work at Capitol Records, I was told to use a certain copyist who worked with most Capitol arrangers, Clyde Balsy, and his partner, Jack Collins. They had their office nearby on Argyle Street. That was where I first met Billy May and Paul Weston, and DeVol. We all worked there whenever there were deadlines to meet. We would finish a score page and turn it over immediately to Clyde or Jack and they would copy out the eighteen parts for the players, and most of the time we made it to the record session on time.

Billy's famous line was "Never trust an arranger who finishes his arrangements two weeks before the session begins. Keep the ink wet for the date."

Frank and I became good friends because we both owned homes in Rancho Mirage, CA, and socialized very often. He was a fine musician, and a very funny man.

While I really enjoyed working on recordings, what I really wanted to do was to get into film scoring. Since television was a new medium and still an unknown entity, I thought that it would be a fleeting fad, and wouldn't last long. In my mind, televison would never replace movies. Movies were a much safer bet. So, if film scoring was what I wanted to do, I felt I would have to have more knowledge about it. I decided to study form and composition with a man reputed to be the best in the business. His name was Mario Castelnuova-Tedesco, the brilliant Italian composer who had earned the reputation in his native Italy as one of the foremost composers for the guitar in the twentieth century.

Like many artists who fled fascism, Castelnuovo-Tedesco ended up in Hollywood, where, with the help of Jascha Heifetz, he landed a contract with Metro-Goldwyn-Mayer as a film composer. Over the next fifteen years, he worked on scores for some 200 films at all the major film studios.

I had heard from some musical colleagues that Mario Tedesco was the man I must go to in order to gain more knowledge about composition and film scoring. When I first met him he was in his eighties. He was a sweet, gentle, and calm man, but was strict in his instruction and expected dedication and hard work from his students. I stayed with him for about a year, and learned to really love him.

While in the midst of working as a freelance arranger for Capitol and other record companies, I got my first break working in television. It was in the year 1954. I had some friends from New York who were out here in Hollywood producing motion pictures. One of them was Maurice Duke. Maurice was handling Mickey Rooney, who was experiencing a "lull" in his film career, but had recently signed to do a thirty-minute weekly television series for NBC called *Hey, Mulligan!*

The show was about the misadventures of Mickey Mulligan, a page at the fictitious International Broadcasting Company in Los Angeles. Undecided about his future, he attends the Academy of Dramatic Arts and by taking various part-time jobs, he struggles to discover his goal in life.

Co-starring on the series were Claire Carleton, who played Mickey's mother, a former burlesque star; Regis Toomey, who played Mickey's father, a policeman; and Carla Balenda, in the role of Mickey's girlfriend, Patricia, a secretary at I. B. C.

Maurice hired me to score the show using a dozen musicians, even though I didn't know anything about scoring pictures at that time, but I learned in a hurry. I asked Irwin Coster, the music editor on the *Hey, Mulligan!* show, to show me the ropes about scoring for television. He helped me tremendously. He showed me about "spotting," how to time different sequences where the music would be included in the film. Each sequence was timed with a stopwatch. This was long before the advent of click tracks. Irwin timed each sequence for me to show me how it was done. He also instructed me on how to sit with the director and producer to decide where in the film sequence the music would be added.

Hey, Mulligan! lasted for one season, from August 28, 1954 to June 4, 1955. I got to meet Mickey Rooney, who was like a big star to me. He had earned his reputation in such films as *Boys Town*, *Men of Boys Town*,

The Human Comedy, National Velvet, all the Andy Hardy movies, and the movies he had played opposite Judy Garland.

Maurice and Mickey parted company and Mickey then hired Red Doff as his manager. I also knew Red from New York. Red hired me to score my first movie with Mickey at Republic Studios called *The Atomic Kid* (1954). Leslie Martinson directed it. The movie was a sci-fi comedy about a uranium prospector who ate a peanut butter sandwich in the desert where atom bomb tests were being conducted. He becomes radio-active and helps the FBI break up an enemy spy ring.

Everybody connected with the film seemed to like what I had done with the score, and so, consequently, I did seven more pictures with Mickey. The others were: *The Twinkle in God's Eye* (1955), in which Mickey plays a priest in a western town; *Baby Face Nelson* (1957), with Mickey in the title role as the 1920s Chicago gangster, with co-stars Carolyn Jones and Sir Cedric Hardwicke; *Andy Hardy Comes Home* (1958), in which Mickey, playing Andy Hardy, is now a grown man with a wife and children, returns to his hometown on a business trip and finds himself getting mixed up in local politics; *The Big Operator* (1959), co-starring Mamie Van Doren and Mel Tormé, where Mickey played a crooked union boss who will stop at nothing to get his way. The studio orchestra and I recorded the title tune as a single that sold pretty well, with the flipside tune being "The Shake."

In fact, in 1957, I arranged and conducted for Mickey an album he recorded for RCA-Victor called *Mickey Rooney Sings George M. Cohan.* The project was a salute to the famed songwriter of Americana, which included his stirring "Yankee Doodle Dandy."

The remaining three Rooney movies include *The Last Mile* (1959), in which jailhouse tensions mount as a killer's (Mickey) execution ap-proaches, and *Platinum High School* (1960), with Mickey investigating the death of his son at an exclusive military academy, whom he has been told died in an accident. The Mick quickly gets in five feet over his eyebrows in trouble. The film also starred Terry Moore and Dan Duryea; and *The Private Lives of Adam and Eve* (1961), a spoof about the Biblical epic of humanity's first parents, Adam and Eve. Mamie Van Doren and Martin Milner co-starred.

Admittingly, these films were not what anyone would call block-busters, but they all provided good credits for me and enabled me to work in other feature films. They were all "B" movies, but they showed up well on my quarterly ASCAP residual statements.

In 1956, I scored the motion picture, *Jaguar*, a jungle epic starring Sabu and a very young Mike Connors, who later starred on the television private investigator series *Mannix*. Mickey Rooney worked as a producer on this film.

Three years later, I also worked on *Girls Town* starring Mamie Van Doren, Mel Tormé, and Ray Anthony. It's a story of a teenage girl who is suspected of killing a young man who tried to rape her. She's sent to Girls Town, a home for young women in trouble with the law, which is run by nuns. The girl then causes all sorts of trouble at the school.

Then Jonie Taps, an ex-song-plugger friend of mine from the old days in New York, recommended me for my next picture. He was the head of the music department at Columbia Pictures. There was an independent picture being made at Columbia called *Safe at Home*. It was a comedy starring New Yankee sluggers Mickey Mantle and Roger Maris. A year earlier, Maris broke Babe Ruth's season home-run record with 61 out-of-the-park hits. So both athletes were big sports celebrities. It's a story about a kid who brags to his Little League buddies that his dad knows Mantle and Maris. Forced to "put up or shut up," the boy goes to the Yankees spring training camp where he is lectured about honesty being the best policy. He returns to face his buddies with the truth to find the entire Little League team invited to camp.

Jonie and the producers of the film were so happy with the job that I did, that Jonie jokingly said that he would like to be my agent.

In 1963, I then worked on *13 Frightened Girls!*, a William Castle film starring Kathy Dunn. The movie was about thirteen girls at a Swiss boarding school. One in particular stirs up trouble on their vacation as they mess with the diplomatic affairs of their elders and get into serious trouble when a Russian spy is discovered murdered. It would the first of three films I did for Castle.

By this time, I had gotten myself a new agent. He was a fine young man named Peter Faith, the son of studio orchestra leader Percy Faith. Peter passed away at a very young age. Just before his untimely death, he obtained three picture deals for me. The first was *Strait-Jacket* (1964), starring Joan Crawford, where she played an insane axe-murderer. This was another Castle-produced film.

The second film Peter secured for me was another Joan Crawford flick, *I Saw What You Did* (1965). It was the last of the three films I did for Castle and it co-starred John Ireland. The suspense-thriller was about two teenage girls who occupy their time by randomly calling strangers by whispering, "I saw what you did," and hanging up. When one of their victims turns out to be a man who has just murdered his wife, he thinks they witnessed the crime and sets out to find the girls and kill them.

The last movie deal Peter made for me was in 1966. It was a Sy Weintraub epic called *Tarzan and the Valley of Gold*, starring Mike Henry. In the movie, Tarzan battles a megalomaniacal millionaire who kidnaps a young boy whom he believes can lead him to a legendary city of gold.

I scored a total of fifteen motion pictures during my career. I would have had at least sixteen except my last one turned out to be the "kiss of death" for me.

It seemed that Columbia had a picture that was "in the can," meaning that all the principle photography had been completed. The movie was called *The Long Ride Home,* a Western starring Glenn Ford and Inger Stevens. The setting is at the close of the Civil War, and a Yankee officer sets out to save his kidnapped fiancée. The consensus of opinion was that the movie was in deep trouble. Directors had been changed in the middle of filming, there were many rewrites on the script and the picture was still lousy. The executive producer was Harry Joe Brown.

Jonie Taps called me in to save the picture with a good musical score, which are the famous last words of producers. They also wanted me to write the main title song in collaboration with Ned Washington, a top lyricist who had written words to such well-known songs as "My Foolish Heart," "Stella By Starlight," "Ghost of a Chance," "When You Wish Upon a Star," "High Noon," and "Rawhide," among others.

Jonie and Mike Frankovich, one of the studio executives, loved the title song Ned and I composed and they made a deal with Eddy Arnold, the famous country-western singer who passed away earlier this year, to sing it over the main title and to also record it for RCA records.

I had seven weeks to write 45 minutes of music. I had plenty of time to work on it and the money was the best I had ever received. I finished the music and I conducted the score on the scoring stage to great acclaim from Harry Joe Brown. I also got raves from Jonie and Frankovich, and the rest of the studio bigwigs. In their opinion, I had really saved the film.

When it came time for the film's preview, Beth and I were there, of course, as was everyone that was connected with the film. What started out in jubilant expectation, ended in disaster. The audience laughed in all the wrong places. They laughed during the dramatic sequences. They hissed at the hero and applauded the villain. God, it was awful! Talk about embarrassing! I wanted to crawl under the table.

A couple days after the preview, I received a telephone call from Jonie Taps. Both he and Frankovich felt that the music was wrong for the picture. I thought that I had written a pretty good score and everyone earlier at the scoring stage had approved.

I asked Jonie if they wanted to change anything and he said, "No, I think that we're going to throw it all out and re-score it with ten guitars and make it a real Western."

So they hired Mundell Lowe, who is a great guitarist. He brought in ten guitars, but that didn't help the picture either. It never played in a theater, but was on television about three weeks later. When it aired, the credits read, "Music by Van Alexander." I called up Jonie Tap.

"Why in the hell are you putting my name on Mundell's score?" I asked.

"That was a big mistake," Jonie replied. "I gave them hell about it in New York. It will be rectified."

The next time the movie aired on TV, the credits read, "Music by Van Alexander with Mundell's score."

By this time I was really hot under the collar. I contacted Jonie once again and told him that if the studio wasn't going to fix it, my attorney would file a lawsuit.

"We'll fix it, don't worry," he said.

We eventually sued Columbia and they paid us. I didn't want my name on Mundell's score and he didn't his on mine.

With such a nightmare, I felt as if I'd never do another picture! I remembered what film composer David Raksin once said: "You're not a full-fledged screen composer until you've had a score thrown out of a picture." The film died a well-deserved death. However, it was the last feature film I ever scored.

After *Baby Face Nelson* was completed, I was asked by singer Guy Mitchell to be the musical director of his thirty-minute weekly musical variety program on NBC called *The Guy Mitchell Show*. The show was broadcast from The Palace Theatre on Vine Street in Hollywood. Guy, whose birth name was Albert Cernik, hit it big as a solo artist at Columbia Records in 1950 after recording "The Roving Kind" and "My Heart Cries for You." He went on to garner six million-selling singles, including "Truly, Truly Fair," "Belle, Belle, My Liberty Bell," "Pittsburgh, Pennsylvania," and, his biggest hit, "Singing the Blues," which was number one for 10 weeks in 1956.

Regulars on the show included singer Delores Hawkins, the Guy Mitchell Singers, and the Teddy Cappy Dancers. While Guy's popularity was at its peak right after "Singing the Blues" broke big, his show only last thirteen weeks, from October 1957 to January 1958.

Guy was very easygoing and fun to be around. He was married at the time to Else Sorenson (a.k.a. Dane Arden), a Danish model who posed in an early 1956 issue of *Playboy* magazine. She was absolutely gorgeous. She'd come to the broadcasts in tight-fitting slacks and blouses and the guys in the band would just drool. Guy telling us in private of his sexual escapades with her only amplified this feeling. Not bashful at all, he would often share in vivid detail what Else and he did that morning in the shower or in the hot tub. He was proud of her, often referring to her as his "good luck charm."

Over the years Guy and I would play golf together whenever I was in Las Vegas. I was saddened to hear of his passing in 1999 from complications following surgery. He was 72.

After *The Guy Mitchell Show* folded, I was then contacted by Irving Friedman, the head of the music department of Screen Gems, a subsidiary of Columbia Pictures, and their television division. My agent, Peter Faith, submitted my name as a music composer and Irving signed me to a non-exclusive contract.

There was a stable of about six composers at Screen Gems which included Allyn Ferguson, Stu Phillips, Hugo Montenegro, Howard Blake, Charles Albertine, and myself. Screen Gems was grinding television shows out like sausages during that period and there was a big demand for music. Whoever was available would do the show. I worked under Ed Forsyth during my time at Screen Gems.

One of the first shows that I worked on for Screen Gems was *The Donna Reed Show*, which ran from 1958 to 1966. Donna won acclaim for her roles in *It's A Wonderful Life* and her Oscar-winning performance as Best Supporting Actress as a prostitute in the 1953 film *From Here to Eternity*. Her television show was another popular 1950s sitcom about a close family, the Stones, consisting of loving homemaker Donna, her pediatrician husband Alex, played by Carl Betz, and their two children, Mary, played by Shelley Fabares, and Paul Peterson as Jeff.

Another show I was involved with was *Dennis the Menace*, starring Jay North as the good-natured but rascally little boy who would give his parents, Herbert Anderson and Gloria Henry, as well as his neighbor, Mr. Wilson, played by Joseph Kearns, fits. *Dennis* aired from 1959 to 1963.

I then worked extensively on *Hazel*, a thirty-minute sitcom starring Shirley Booth in which she played a live-in maid and her misadventures in trying to solve crises in the household of her attorney boss George Baxter, played by Don DeFore. *Hazel* ran on NBC from 1961 to 1965, and then went into syndication on CBS from 1965 to 1966.

Another Screen Gems hit show that I worked on was *I Dream of Jeannie*. Hugo Montenegro wrote the show's catchy theme. When *I Dream of Jeannie* aired on NBC from 1965 to 1970, it gave the censors fits. The show starred Barbara Eden as a female genie, and Larry Hagman as an astronaut who becomes her master, with whom she falls in love and eventually marries. Barbara would often show off her voluptuous figure.

I did two shows in 1966, a two-part special called "The Girl Who Never Had a Birthday." Part one aired on November 14, where Jeannie is sad that she doesn't know her birthday and she starts to vanish feet first. The second part aired the following week, on November 21, in which Tony (Larry Hagman) runs around trying to get Jeannie's birthday from his friend, Roger, who had it sent to Alaska.

Thirty-eight years after it's been off the air, *I Dream of Jeannie* continues to have a cult following today.

I also worked in 1966 on three episodes of *Bewitched*, a sitcom broadcast on ABC from 1964 to 1972 for eight seasons. The show starred Elizabeth Montgomery, a housewife named Samantha, who is half-mortal and half-witch who is married to her mortal husband Darrin, played by Dick York (1964–1969), and later Dick Sargent (1969–1972), and , as Samantha's antaganistic witch mother.

My first episode was called "And Then There Were Three," airing on January 13, in which Samantha gives birth to Tabitha and Darrin meets Serena, Samantha's spiteful cousin, for the first time.

The second episode, "The Leprechaun," aired March 17 in time for St. Patrick's Day, and involved Samantha helping a leprechaun from Darrin's side of the family.

The final episode was entitled "The Short, Happy Circuit of Aunt Clara," which aired on October 11. The good-natured but magically clumsy Aunt Clara, played by Marion Lorne, knocks out the entire Eastern Seaboard's electricity with her magic. Her only hope is her old boyfriend Ocky, who can keep the lights on by having his arms raised.

Bewitched continues to be seen throughout the world in syndication and it is the longest-running supernatural-themed sitcom of the 1960s–1970s.

I also worked a few episodes on *The Farmer's Daughter*, which aired on ABC from 1963 to 1966. This was a half-hour sitcom about Katy Holstrum (Inger Stevens), a Swedish farm girl who is governess to the children of widowed Congressman Glen Morley (William Windom). It was tragic news to hear of Inger's apparent suicide of a drug overdose in 1970. She was only 35 years old.

While all these Screen Gems television shows may seem "corny" by today's standards, many of them were of such high quality in their day that they were either nominated and/or won Emmy or Golden Globe awards. Many of them are still in syndication and are shown around the world and continually show up on my ASCAP statements.

Having the varied background I had by working in the recording industry and for television and in feature films, I was stylistically like a chameleon, where I could blend from one setting to the next. Someone once called me a "journeyman arranger." That's a high compliment. In many ways, I feel like I've done it all.

However, two important and very satisfying chapters in my professional career were unfolding during this period. They had to do with Gordon MacRae and Dean Martin, two pop singers/actors whose stars shone brightly and colorfully as the Aurora Borealis.

An early publicity photo of myself in 1938 as a budding bandleader.

Above and Below: My band in Atlantic City, New Jersey, in the spring of 1940. I'm pictured in the middle wearing a white blazer. Our band vocalist Phyllis Kenny is on my left. Butch Stone is pictured third from my right.

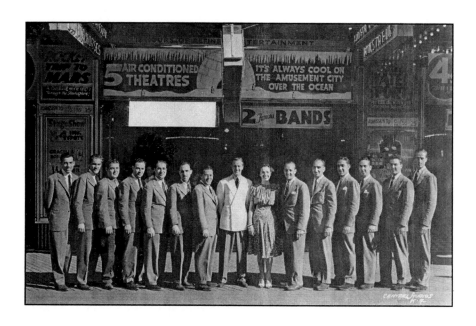

Above left: Addressing the audience at Loew's State Theater in 1940 in New York City, while bantering with bassist Leroy "Slam" Stewart at the same venue, (Below right).

Above: My band playing at Loew's State Theater in 1940.

My Waterloo: A lit up marquee of the Paramount Theater where my band played in 1940. Unfortunately, the movie that was playing was a dud and as a result, we lasted one quick week at the famed theater. I disbanded my full-time band shortly thereafter.

Left: A photo of me with bandleader Hal Kemp in 1940 shortly before he died in a tragic automobile accident. Hal had a terrific band and he died way too young.

Above: My band on the Boardwalk in Atlantic City, New Jersey, in 1940. L to R are: Sandy Block, Lenny Hartman, Butch Stone, Bert Haas, Bill Schallen, Sol Kane, Phyllis Kenny, me, Harry Pelsinger, Ralph Kessler, Irv Cottler, Ben Finklestein, Don Jacoby.

Above: My beloved wife Beth and I strolling on the Boardwalk in Atlantic City, New Jersey, in 1938. Don't we make an adorable couple?

One of my first recording sessions in Hollywood in 1947 as a bandleader: I was leading a group of all-star musicians for Irving Mills on his ARA Records. Pictured in the band are saxophonists Butch Stone, Lucky Thompson, Stan Getz, Clint Neagley and Eddie Rosa. Not pictured are Frank Beach, Chuck Peterson, Charlie Shavers, Sid Harris, Si Zenter, Charles Maxson, Jimmy Rowles, Tony Rizzi, Arnold Fishkind, and Don Lamond.

I was happy to be writing out an arrangement for Mickey Rooney and Helen Forrest. I later scored music for Mickey's TV show *Hey! Mulligan* and for eight of his motion pictures.

What a thrill it was for me to work on two albums at Capitol Records with the great Jack Teagarden! Here I am with Jackson "T" in 1956, after recording *This Is Teagarden,* our first album.

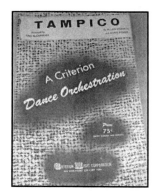

Left: Just a sample of one of the many stock arrangements for dance bands I did that was published by Criterion Music Corporation. My dear friend Mickey Goldsen owned Criterion Music and gave me work when I was struggling to get by in 1946, after moving to Los Angeles. I will be forever grateful for Mickey's graciousness.

Above: Working with the fabulous Kay Starr at Capitol Records in 1959, on *Movin'*, the first of four albums we made together. Over the years Kay has become a very dear friend.

Left: A sample cover of the many children's albums I worked on at Capitol Records with the gifted but zany Mel Blanc, known as "The Man of a Thousand Voices." Mel was the voice for all the Warner Bros. cartoon characters including Daffy Duck, Sylvester the Cat, Tweedy Pie, Elmer Fudd, Speedy Gonzalez, and everyone's favorite rabbit, Bugs Bunny.

CHAPTER SEVEN

MY BUDDY

Back in my band days, there was a young publicist who did some work for me whose name was Marty Melcher. In 1950, Marty and his partner, Dick Dorso, formed a booking agency called Century Artists. One of their clients was a young, good-looking singer-actor named Gordon MacRae.

Gordon was probably best remembered for his starring roles in the film versions of the Rodgers and Hammerstein musicals *Oklahoma!* (1955) and *Carousel* (1956). Born Albert Gordon MacRae in East Orange, New Jersey, he was the son of radio star "Wee Willie" MacRae, and his concert pianist mother.

Shortly after his graduation from high school, he won a singing contest sponsored by *Picture Magazine*. The prize was a two-week engagement at the 1939 New York World's Fair performing with the Harry James and Les Brown bands. Unfortunately, I don't recall Gordon performing there at the time. Shortly afterwards, he worked as a singer with Horace Heidt's band in New York City.

In May 1941, he wed actress Sheila Margot Stephens; they would have four children: Meredith, Heather, Gar and Bruce. Of the four, Meredith and Heather MacRae would both pursue acting careers.

During World War II, Gordon joined the Army Air Force, serving as a navigator for two years. At the end of the war, he returned to New York City, where he made his Broadway debut in the show *Junior Miss*. In 1946, he appeared in the Broadway show *Three to Make Ready,* in which a Capitol Records talent scout saw him and signed him to a long-term recording contract. Gordon would stay with Capitol Records for the next twenty years. During the late 1940s he recorded many successful duets with Jo Stafford, including "'A'- You're Adorable," "Say Something

Sweet to Your Sweetheart," and an album of religious music that included the hymn, "Whispering Hope."

In October 1948, Gordon starred on the radio show, *The Railroad Hour*, which aired on ABC. The show moved to NBC in October 1949 and continued until June of 1954. It presented operettas and musical dramatizations, all starring Gordon with many different leading ladies. Also in 1948, he signed a seven-year contract with Warner Brothers, and made his film-acting debut in *The Big Punch* opposite Lois Maxwell.

His next film was a musical, *Look for the Silver Lining* (1949), in which his singing talent made him the lead actor; and five fondly remembered films with Doris Day beginning in 1950 with *Tea for Two*. Later that same year, Gordon and Doris, along with James Cagney and Virginia Mayo, starred in musical comedy *The West Point Story*.

The remaining MacRae-Day films include *Starlift* (1951), *On Moonlight Bay* (1951), and *By the Light of the Silvery Moon* (1953).

When I was scuffling to get my name recognized in the music industry in Los Angeles, I called Marty Melcher because I knew at that time he was a pretty big agent. I asked if he could do anything for me. He was producing pictures at the time with Gordon and his soon-to-be-wife, Doris Day. He told me he couldn't do anything for me at that time. I was disappointed.

Years later when I was doing pretty well in pictures and in television, I saw Marty and he said to me, "See, Van, you never needed me after all." That was a famous quote of his.

"Well, I needed you then, Marty," I shot back.

Even Mickey Goldsen was critical of Marty's failure to help me.

"That SOB, he could have helped you when you needed it," he said.

Shortly after I signed on at Capitol Records, I worked with Gordon on a number of singles in late 1951 and early 1952. It was our first meeting together. We recorded about sixteen songs during this period; things like "Green Acres and Purple Mountains," "My Love," "Laughing at Love," "Mansion Over the Hilltop," "Peace in the Valley," and "Nine Hundred Miles."

I was impressed by his easy-going nature and his magnificent voice. Oh, what a voice! We hit it off together very well.

Gordon and I did a few more singles together on Capitol in 1953 and 1954 with a fine cover of Tony Bennett's hit version of "Stranger in Paradise," "Never in a Million Years," "Stuffy," "Cara Mia," and "Count Your Blessings."

In addition, Gordon and June Hutton, formerly of the Pied Pipers, recorded a handful of duet singles with me: "Open Arms," "Tik-A-Tee, Tik-A-Tay," and "Tell Me That You Love Me."

When Gordon was booked to do some nightclub dates to cash in on his movie popularity, it was then that Marty Melcher called me asking me to meet with Gordon because he needed an arranger/conductor. It was right after he made *By the Light of the Silvery Moon* with Doris Day.

I had built a pretty good rapport with Gordon when I worked with him on the singles that we recorded on Capitol. Gordon didn't have a regular musical director. He usually worked with the studio orchestra when making films and recordings. When he did his radio show, *The Railroad Hour*, Carmen Dragon usually conducted the music for that program.

A few days after Marty had me meet Gordon at his Century Artists office, Gordon invited me to his beautiful ranch-style home just off of Laurel Canyon Boulevard in Studio City. I remember this vividly. It was about 10 A.M., and Gordon and I were talking in the den about what he wanted to be included in his nightclub act when in comes Sheila wearing a flimsy, see-through nightgown. She let out a scream when she saw me. This was our first meeting and she yelled at Gordon, "Why didn't you tell me you had a guest?" We all laughed about our initial meeting afterwards for many years.

For Gordon's nightclub act, I wrote charts for him based on material he sang in his movies as well as the Henry I. Marshall and Stanley Murphy tune, "Be My Little Bumble Bee," that Doris originally sang in *Silvery Moon*.

Over a year later, I received another call from Marty. Gordon had just finished filming the smash hit, *Oklahoma!* at 20th Century-Fox, which had established him as a pretty big star. Gordon played the role of Curly, a good-natured ranch hand who tries to court screen newcomer Shirley Jones against the interests of Rod Steiger, the movie's "heavy." Gordon was magnificent in the role, setting female hearts aflutter with such standards as "Surrey with the Fringe on Top" and "People Will Say We're in Love," and especially when he sang "Oh, What a Beautiful Mornin'"— his big, baritone voice resonating wonderfully as he rode so proudly on horseback through the cornfields.

Gordon was once again booked to go out on personal appearance tours and he needed a conductor-arranger. Since our earlier professional association worked out well, Gordon asked Marty to have me come aboard full time, which I eagerly accepted.

Gordon long had his eye on playing the lead role of Billy Bigelow, the irresponsible carnival barker who returns from an early death in an attempt to find redemption, in the film version of *Carousel*. Gordon knew he was perfect for the part as he was well-versed with the Broadway version, but the film execs at 20th Century-Fox instead signed on Frank Sinatra to play the lead. Gordon was more than disappointed.

A few weeks into the film's production, Gordon was performing at the Cal-Neva Lodge in Lake Tahoe when he received a telephone call from 20th Century-Fox. Sinatra walked out on the picture because each scene had to be shot twice (once in 35mm, once in 55mm) and he didn't want to repeat scenes over again, so the studio asked Gordon if he would be the film's last-minute replacement. With an elated and resounding, "Yes!" that echoed throughout the backstage dressing rooms, the "new" Billy Bigelow flew to Maine to join the film crew after we had finished the Cal-Neva date.

Three weeks after Sinatra left, it was announced that production technicians found a way to film scenes only once on 55mm, and then transfer it onto 35mm. Such a fortuitous event as Sinatra's departure from the picture allowed Gordon to play what would be his best film role, and to sing *Carousel's* immortal "Soliloquy." Gordon received critical acclaim for his portrayal, while once again playing opposite Shirley Jones. Ironically, *Carousel* turned out to be a box-office flop, but the film's soundtrack album did become a national bestseller. It topped out at the number two position and remained charted for 59 weeks.

Gordon revealed years later that during the filming of *Carousel*, he was "picked up for drunk driving." Marty helped to squash such news from the press at the time of the incident in order to protect Gordon's career. However, this was just the beginning of Gordon's many bouts of heavy drinking that would ultimately plague his career.

Once Gordon finished filming *Carousel*, he moved to television with his own show, *The Gordon MacRae Show*, which lasted only one season. It was a 15-minute musical variety show on NBC that aired from March 5, 1956 to August 27, 1956. I had a great time working as the show's musical director.

Gordon also guest-starred on a number of television shows such as *The Jimmy Durante Show*, *Lux Video Theatre*, and *Hallmark Hall of Fame*. We also did a few one-hour specials, one being from the Fontainebleau Hotel in Miami.

As a result of his television appeal, Gordon garnered two Prime Time Emmy nominations for Best Male Singer in 1955 and 1956.

Surprisingly, when I did *The Guy Mitchell Show* for thirteen weeks, it never interfered with what Gordon and I were doing. However, when I was working on a few pictures at Columbia there were some instances where our schedules did conflict. When I couldn't do a four-week Las Vegas date with Gordon and Shelia, I got them a substitute, Dominic Frontiere. During another scheduling conflict, I had Don Bagely, a good friend of mine who used to play bass with Les Brown and in other Big Bands, to sub for me. He was a good arranger and conductor.

During my association with Gordon, I wrote and conducted thirteen albums for him at Capitol Records, the first being in 1956, with *The Best Things in Life Are Free*. Others were *Cowboy's Lament* (1957); *Motion Picture Soundstage* (1957); *Gordon MacRae in Concert* (1958); *Seasons of Love* (1959); *Songs for an Evening at Home* (1959); *Hallowed Be Thy Name* (1960); *Our Love Story* (1960); *The Desert Song* (1963); *New Moon* (1963); *The Student Prince* (1963); *Kismet* (1964); and *If She Walked into My Life* (1966).

My personal favorite album is *Gordon MacRae in Concert*. The title is misleading, as this was not a "live" performance album. The twelve-song studio-recorded project featured some of Gordon's most powerful renditions of show-stopping numbers such as "Begin the Beguine," "Ol' Man River," "I Believe," "Danny Boy," and "Without a Song." Stylistically, it's a wonderfully diverse album.

I can honestly say that working with Gordon was one of the most pleasurable and profitable experiences of my career. Working with him really cemented my career at Capitol Records as well. Unfortunately, Gordon was never a big record seller outside of his movie soundtracks. The Capitol producers tried everything with him. Even with his glorious voice, he couldn't sell records. He lacked a certain "something." We tried to do some contemporary things with him but he didn't have that "Sinatra beat," that "Sinatra feel," which seemed to be a key ingredient in trying to create a "hip" offering.

In actuality, Gordon and I were quite a team. We played all the best hotels and clubs in the country: The Waldorf-Astoria in New York City, The Fairmont in San Francisco, The Chez Paree in Chicago, The Desert Inn in Las Vegas, The Royal Hawaiian in Honolulu, The Cocoanut Grove in The Ambassador Hotel in Los Angeles, The Caribe Hilton in Puerto Rico...the list goes on and on.

When Gordon first started doing nightclubs, on rare occasions he would introduce Sheila, his wife, at the end of his act and she would do a couple of impressions of some of the current personalities. She was very good and got good reviews.

Little by little Gordon gave her more and more time in the act, so much so that a comic once said, "Is Sheila singing *Oklahoma* yet?"

When Shelia teamed up with Gordon, she would always try to incorporate something spectacular into the act that would make for a good show. One such idea involved aerial theatrics. *Peter Pan* was a big hit on Broadway because of the genius of Peter Foy who invented a prop that looked like a big howitzer gun that could sustain a person who wore a harness to simulate someone flying, as little Mary Martin did. Sheila thought it would be a great thing for her to do in the act. So at no little cost, Shelia brought Peter Foy and his equipment to come their home where they had a pretty good-sized studio for rehearsals. For three weeks prior to going to the Desert Inn in Vegas, Sheila got into the harness and practiced flying around the room.

To make a long story short, we opened in Las Vegas and Mr. Foy and his machine were flying Sheila very low out over the audience, all of whom who are ducking and screaming and covering their heads. After the first performance the bosses of the casino came backstage and said, "You can't be doing this, it's too risky. Mary Martin is a little woman. Sheila, you're too big for this." Sheila was heartbroken besides being black and blue from days of rehearsing.

The next day around the pool, an airplane flew over kind of low and comedian Jackie Leonard shouted out, "There goes Sheila Stephens."

In all honesty, Sheila developed into a great impersonator and a fairly good singer and helped propel the act into one of the greatest nightclub acts around. She is perhaps best remembered for playing Alice Kramden, the long-suffering but sassy wife of bus driver Ralph Kramden (played by Jackie Gleason) on the musical-comedy color episodes of *The Honeymooners* on *The Jackie Gleason Show* from 1966 to 1970. Her final appearance as Alice came in a 1973 Gleason special on CBS.

What most people didn't know was that while Sheila loved being in the act with Gordon, she really did it as sort of self-preservation. She knew Gordon wasn't too dedicated and that his drinking and gambling were always problematic. She believed that if she was with him, she might have a certain degree of control over him. It was wishful thinking, but it never happened.

Sometimes Gordon's behaviors with alcohol and gambling got downright ugly. We got to be very close friends until his drinking started to take over, then we had difficulties.

One instance I vividly remember was the closing night after we did three weeks at the Desert Inn in Las Vegas. Gordon and Sheila, and Beth and I had planned to drive home to Los Angeles after the last show. We were all packed, dressed and ready to go. Gordon was wearing his beautiful vicuña coat, but he had a couple of drinks and said, "I'll be with you guys in a few minutes," and proceeded to the crap table.

He promptly lost a few thousand dollars, and wouldn't leave. We three were waiting and waiting. Someone said to Sheila, "Why don't you just go over and pull him away from the table?"

I'll never forget what she said: "It's one thing to lose my money, but I will never lose my dignity."

We didn't want to leave without Gordon, so we three gave up and went to bed, thinking we'd head out early the following morning. Early next morning I went downstairs to the casino. There was nobody playing and I asked one of the pit bosses what happened to Gordon and if he knew where he was. He told me Gordon was in the men's room.

I rushed there and Gordon was standing at a urinal still wearing his vicuña coat and greeted me with "Hi ya, buddy."

I said, "What happened last night? Did you get out without losing too much?"

He turned around to face me and with a silly grin on his face, he put both his hands in both pockets and said, "I've got every fucking black chip in the joint." Black chips were each worth a hundred dollars.

I said, "That's wonderful, Gordy, now let's get the hell out of here."

Gordon said, "Hell, I can't go now. I'm on a roll!"

Well, you can guess what happened.

Sheila, Beth and I left him there and drove back to LA. Gordon gave back all his winnings, which we figured were about $25,000, and he dropped an additional $10,000. He came home later that day.

Another incident involving Gordon's problematic drinking occurred after we had worked together, but remained close friends. In 1978, Gordon called and asked if I would be interested in playing golf in the Greater Greensboro Pro-Am Tournament in North Carolina. Gordon was going to play and then sing at the banquet after the tournament. He wanted me to accompany him. Beth was also invited and we both excitedly and enthusiastically accepted.

I had a ball! I played a practice round at Forest Oaks Country Club with Fred De Cordova, the Emmy Award-winning producer of *The Tonight Show*, and a couple of other guys from *The Tonight Show*. The next day I was in a group with the great Lee Elder, who became the first African American to play in the Masters Tournament in 1975. Lee, of course, paved the way for the new young golfing sensation, Tiger Woods.

I was a 17 handicap at the time and I shot an 84 that day. I sank a couple of 30-foot putts and I have the scoring card and the 6th-place winning plaque hanging on the wall in my office to prove it! Lee referred to me as his "California Pro" and I was feeling pretty full of myself.

Beth got to meet some wonderful people who were working as volunteers at the event. One couple in particular, Ren and Renee Thornhill, showed her all the historical sights in Winston-Salem and the neighboring towns during our week's stay. We corresponded with them for quite a few years.

The only drag of the whole event was that poor Gordon had too much to drink before the closing party and was unable to sing at all. Singer Howard Keel was there and he offered to sing. He got up and sang, of all songs, "Oh, What a Beautiful Mornin'" from *Oklahoma!* Gordon stood up and made matters worse by shouting, "Hey, that's *my* song!" It was quite embarrassing for everyone. Beth and I were mortified. It brought back so many troublesome memories for me of Gordon's alcoholic episodes.

However, there were many pleasurable times I had with Gordon. One memorable moment that stands out was when the MacRaes had an engagement at the Caribe Hilton in Puerto Rico. Pablo Casals, one of the most famous cellists in the world, lived in Puerto Rico. Gordon thought it would be great if he, Shelia and I could get to meet him.

Unbeknownst to us, many other people had the same idea. In fact, there were so many people who wanted to meet Casals that you had to make an appointment to see him.

We did just that and we still had to wait in an ante room for quite a while. It was sort of like having an audience with the pope.

We finally got in to see him and Casals told Gordon that he understood he was a singer and asked what kind of music he sang. Opera? Casals evidentially had never heard of Gordon, even after *Oklahoma!* and *Carousel*. Well, Gordon hemmed and hawed and there was sort of a lull in the conversation.

After a few awkward moments, I asked Señor Casals if he was familiar with Alfred Wallenstein, first cellist of the Los Angeles Symphony. Of course Casals knew him! He thought he was a fine musician. I then told Señor Casals a musicians' anecdote.

When Mr. Wallenstein was first cellist in the New York Philharmonic Orchestra, he would play his part impeccably, but he would never look at the conductor. One day during a break in the rehearsal, the conductor took him aside and asked him what his life-long ambition was. Mr. Wallenstein told him straight out that he wanted nothing more than to be a conductor of a great symphony orchestra. The conductor looked him straight in the eye and told him that he hoped he wouldn't have a Wallenstein sitting in front of him.

Upon hearing that Casals slapped his knee and let out a hearty laugh, which broke the ice. We spent the next fifteen minutes in a nice relaxed atmosphere. Gordon later thanked me for telling Casals that story. It saved the entire afternoon.

Before we left, I did manage to get an autographed picture of Señor Casals, which is part of my collection of over 125 or so pictures of people that I have either worked with or simply admired through the years.

Because Gordon and I had developed such a close friendship, as did both our families, we did a lot of family things together. One of the first activities was going on a cruise. Sometime in the mid-1950s Ted Grouya, who wrote the Herb Jeffries' hit "Flamingo," was the shaker and mover behind the Lurline Cruises to Hawaii. He promoted a cruise deal that was called "Sail with the Stars." He booked Gordon along with Dorothy Dandridge, and the three Crosby boys—Dennis, Gary, and Phil—along with their wives. But Gordon said, "I can't go without Sheila, and our kids. And I'll need my conductor, Van Alexander, and he won't go without his wife and kids." Sheila also insisted that her mother and her companion must go, as well as Sheila's secretary, Shirley Vaughn. Grouya and the Lurline execs OK'd the additional entourage. Gordon only had to sing once on the way over, and then sing one night at the Royal Hawaiian Hotel. It was a marvelous trip, but it was the first and last "Sail with the Stars" trip. Ted Grouya lost his job, and the Lurline Cruises lost a bundle.

The MacRaes and the Alexanders would often spend time together at Lake Tahoe: swimming and boating on the lake during the summer, and having a ball frolicking in the snow during the winter. We would take our kids along on tours whenever possible, and in so doing, we tried to provide a normal family life.

Gordon showed his abiding friendship toward me in a special way when my father died. It was 1956 and I was conducting the *Gordon MacRae Show* when I got the call from my brother David that our father had suddenly died as a result of suffering a massive stroke. There was nothing I could do at that particular moment, so I finished the show and then made arrangements to travel back to New York to be with my mother. Dad and Mom had made many friends over the years through their associations with the Masons and the Eastern Star, so there was quite a crowd at Dad's funeral. To my surprise and gratitude, in walked Gordon. It was a sincere gesture of his love for me and his presence was a welcomed comfort to my mother.

During the time of my association with Gordon, I experienced a "blast from the past" that really hit me for a loop. I was playing with the MacRaes at the Diplomat Hotel in Hollywood, Florida. Since my name always appeared in all of the publicity promos, I periodically would receive telephone calls or notes from old friends who heard that I was in town. This particular time I received a phone call from Frieda Amchin, one of my former high-school girlfriends who was voted the prettiest girl in our senior class.

Frieda told me over the phone that she was visiting relatives just 100 miles up the Florida coast and that she would love to come see me. I explained to her that we were closing that night and we would be leaving for California the next morning. She insisted that she would drive down to Hollywood early in the morning with her daughter and we could have a quick cup of coffee. Beth OK'd it, so I told her that I would love to see her.

We got to sleep pretty late that evening after closing the show. The telephone rang in our hotel room at 7 a.m., waking Beth and me out of a very sound sleep. It was Frieda. She and her daughter were waiting for me downstairs in the hotel coffee shop. I told her I'd be right down.

I entered the coffee shop and I didn't see any Frieda, at least the Frieda I had envisioned in my mind. In fact, there were only two people in the whole place…a little old lady, all gray and wrinkled, and a young girl. Oh, no, I thought to myself. It couldn't be…or could it? With much trepidation I approached the booth where the two females were sitting and in a slightly crackling voice I said, "Frieda?"

My worst fears were confirmed. It was Frieda. I couldn't believe my eyes! How could this be? Here was the girl who was once voted the prettiest girl in the senior class and now she looked like Maria Ouspenskaya, the Russian-born stage and screen actress best remembered for her role as the old Gypsy woman in the horror films *The Wolf Man* (1941) and *Frankenstein Meets The Wolf Man* (1943).

We had our cup of coffee and reminisced. Frieda had changed her name to Jade Pasteur and had been a fairly well-known portrait artist living in Desert Hot Springs, California, just north of Palm Springs. She had been married and divorced twice and was currently a widow.

I brought her up to date on my life and about my family. She offered to paint portraits of our daughters, Lynn and Joyce, but Beth said not to get involved, and Beth hasn't been wrong in all our years of marriage. That was the last time I had any contact with Frieda.

Gordon and Shelia had four beautiful children and our kids and their kids sort of grew up together. The oldest of the MacRae children was Meredith, next came Heather, then Gar, and finally, Bruce. Meredith and Heather were the talented singers/actresses in the family. Meredith, who also co-starred on TV's *Petticoat Junction* and *My Three Sons* during the 1960s and early 1970s, and had won an Emmy for her work as a talk show host on *Mid-Morning Los Angeles*, died in 2000 of a brain tumor. She was 56.

Gordon and Shelia divorced in 1967 and a few months later Gordon married Elizabeth Lamberti Schrafft. In the late 1970s, he conquered his alcoholism and went on to counsel other alcoholics. Gordon continued to act in a few pictures and television shows before suffering a stroke in 1982. He died in 1986 of pneumonia, from complications due to cancer of the mouth and jaw, at his home in Lincoln, Nebraska, at the age of 64.

I was profoundly saddened to hear of Gordon's passing. He was a dear friend. I really miss him, even to this day. He sort of straightened out at the end of his life, but it was a little too late. He was also a big gambler. In the beginning, he'd make $25,000 a week in Las Vegas, but would lose it all at the tables. Gordon had to pay taxes on the money he won and he ended up owing the government over a million dollars. Sheila's still around. I talk with her occasionally, but she's having a bit of a financial struggle at this time in her life. It's a sad story, considering all of the money the two of them made.

CHAPTER EIGHT

EVERYBODY LOVES SOMEBODY

Many times, things that look like a disaster turn out to be a blessing in disguise. Right after the catastrophe I had with the film *The Long Ride Home*, I received a call from my dear friend Les Brown, who was the musical director for *The Dean Martin Show*. He asked me if I'd like to come over and do some arrangements for the show. There were a couple of other guys also doing arrangements for the show at the same time. I enthusiastically took Les up on his kind offer and went to work for him and Dean.

When I joined the show, Dean Martin had been a household name in the entertainment industry for the past 20 years. In 1946, Jerry Lewis and he collaborated together to form the hottest and funniest comedy team around at the time. After their break up ten years later, Dean was already a major recording star with such hits as "That's Amore," "Sway," "Volare," "Mambo Italiano," "Memories Are Made of This," and his biggest hit and subsequent theme song, "Everybody Loves Somebody." He epitomized the word "cool."

Born Dino Paul Crocetti in 1917, in Steubenville, Ohio, Dean started out as a boxer. After achieving some minor success as a pugilist, he later sang with local bands. Billing himself as "Dino Martini," he got his first break working for the Ernie McKay Orchestra, a territory band out of Columbus, Ohio. In the early 1940s, he started singing for bandleader Sammy Watkins, who led a band based in Cleveland, at which time Watkins suggested that he change his name to Dean Martin.

In October 1941, Dean married Elizabeth Anne McDonald, and during their marriage (ended by divorce in 1949), they had four children. He later married Jeanne Biegger and together had three children. The couple divorced in 1972. Dean married a final time to then-26-

year-old Catherine Hawn. Before their marriage dissolved three years later, Dean adopted Hawn's daughter.

After serving in the Army for a year during World War II, Dean was discharged for medical reasons.

Dean bummed around on the East Coast nightclub circuit until he met Jerry Lewis at the Glass Hat Club in New York, where both men were performing. Dean and Jerry formed a fast friendship which led to their participation in each other's acts and the ultimate formation of a music-comedy team, calling themselves "Martin and Lewis."

Martin and Lewis' official debut together occurred at Atlantic City's 500 Club on July 24, 1946. Their success at the 500 Club eventually led to a triumphant run at New York's Copacabana. Hollywood beckoned Dean and Jerry to national stardom, making sixteen movies together.

As the saying goes, "all good things must come to an end," and that also held true for Dean and Jerry. Their act broke up in 1956, ten years to the day after the first official teaming. Dean went his way and Jerry went his; each with respective successes in forging a solo career.

Dean continued to record and star in films. He recorded more than 100 albums and 600 songs. His signature tune, "Everybody Loves Somebody," knocked The Beatles' "A Hard Day's Night" out of the number-one spot in the USA in 1964.

His critically acclaimed film credits include *Rio Bravo* (1959), *Ocean's Eleven* (1960), *4 for Texas* (1963), *Robin and the 7 Hoods* (1964), *The Sons of Katie Elder* (1965), *5 Card Stud* (1968), and *Airport* (1970). Dean also starred in and co-produced a series of four *Matt Helm* superspy comedy adventures.

As Dean's solo career grew, he and Frank Sinatra became close friends. In the late 1950s and early 1960s, Dean and Sinatra, along with friends Joey Bishop, Peter Lawford, and Sammy Davis, Jr., formed the legendary "Rat Pack," so called by the public. The Rat Pack was legendary for their Las Vegas performances. Their act consisted of each singing individual numbers, duets and trios, along with much seemingly improvised slapstick and chatter.

In 1965, Dean launched his own 60-minute variety show featuring comedy and song. It was first aired over NBC on September 16, 1965 and ran until May 24, 1974. Dean exploited his public image as a lazy, carefree boozer. It was there that he perfected his famous laid-back persona of a half-drunk crooner suavely hitting on beautiful women with hilarious remarks that would get anyone else slapped, and later, making snappy if slurred remarks about fellow celebrities during his famous roasts. Few entertainers worked as hard to make what they were doing look so easy.

Regulars on the show included Ken Lane, Dean's pianist; the Golddiggers, originally called "Dean's Girls," a group of a dozen talented and beautiful young ladies between eighteen and twenty-two years of age assembled by Greg Garrison, the show's producer, through open auditions; the beautiful Ding-A-Ling Sisters (Lynn Latham, Tara Leigh, Helen Funai, and Jayne Kennedy), a spin-off of the Golddiggers; and comedians Dom DeLuise and Nipsey Russell, who were featured in the regular skit "At the Barbershop," where Dean would get a "trim" by barbers Dom or Nipsey while zany discussions on various world affairs between them would ensue. All the music for the show was conducted by Les Brown.

Les and I have been good friends for many years, long before either of us knew Dean Martin. We socialized quite often. His first wife, Claire, and my Beth were very close.

When Dean's show started, Dean insisted on using Les as the conductor. Greg Garrison went along with it but for some reason or other he never "dug" Les. I would conduct the show in Les' absence.

I remember when Les was overseas with Bob Hope entertaining the troops; Peggy Lee was booked to be on the show. She came into the studio and said, "Where's Les Brown?"

Greg said to her, with me standing right there, "Today's your lucky day, Peggy. Van Alexander is conducting for you."

Les was cognizant of Greg's feelings but never once mentioned it to me. Although at times Les may have felt a bit chagrined, it never affected our friendship. I really loved Les. He was one of the "good" guys.

In addition to writing arrangements for the show, my job was to be in the control booth and making sure the band was properly balanced. I sat next to Bill Livitsky, the audio engineer who was a very talented music-minded mixer. I would cue him as to what was happening in the band so that he could be ready to bring up the woodwinds or to soften the brass as needed.

One day, after the orchestra and principal players were well rehearsed, we started taping and in one number the lead trumpet player hit a "clam," a musician's term for a wrong note. It was heard over Florence Henderson's vocal solo, and very noticeable. Les looked up at the booth and I motioned to him to cut, which he did. Well, I guess we did the wrong thing because Greg was livid.

"No one says, 'Cut,' except me!" Greg barked. "We're not making records, for Christ's sake!"

That was the last time either of us ever said anything about wrong notes. Greg didn't care, but Les sure did.

Greg was a very shrewd but extremely gifted producer. He got his start in television in the late 1940s directing Milton Berle on his popular *Texaco Star Theater*. He went on to produce early live TV game shows. His first taste of real success came with the five-season run of *The Kate Smith Show* in the early 1950s. He later was one of six rotating directors on John Forsythe's popular *Bachelor Father*. He also directed *Your Show of Shows*, the comedy-variety program that starred Sid Caesar, Imogene Coca, Carl Reiner and Howard Morris. Greg also holds the distinction of having directed one of the 1960 Nixon-Kennedy debates, setting a standard for the political electoral process that continues to this day. He directed nearly 4,000 shows in his career.

Greg was largely responsible for the enormous success of *The Dean Martin Show*; somewhat of a miracle due to Dean's contractual restrictions he worked under. Dean never rehearsed with guest stars. The only way he agreed to do the TV show was if he could come in on the day of the taping, which to all of us seemed ridiculous. Perry Como would rehearse for two or three weeks for an hour show. Greg went along with Dean because with Dean being a naturally funny man, he figured the spontaneity would produce more laughs than things that were rehearsed.

When singer Engelbert Humperdink was a guest, Dean never saw or spoke to him before he was introduced on camera. Dean slapped him on the back and said, "Hi Ya, Hump! How's your Dink?" which brought the house down.

Greg believed that his number one function was to keep Dean happy at all costs and he employed overbooking as a means to replace guest stars and lesser acts should they balk. Guest stars who learned to work within these unique restrictions enjoyed frequent encore appearances; those that didn't weren't seen with Dean on TV again.

Greg required guest stars to rehearse with stand-ins (often himself and assistant director/producer Lee Hale) and would seldom tolerate dissent. Making it look easy was hard work, but Greg also understood the importance of surrounding himself with high-caliber production talent and ran each production with speed and precision.

Dean had someone record the rehearsal on cassette tape so he could listen to it in his car going to and from the golf course. Dean prided himself on memorizing whole scripts—not merely his own lines. If a female singing star was booked on the show, we would tape an audio cassette with Lee Hale and one of the girl singers, usually Melissa MacKay, singing the duet. Dean learned it sort of halfway and on the day of the taping if he made a mistake everyone laughed and they'd do it again. Dean wasn't really too dedicated but he was likeable and charming and would say, "Hey, whatever you want, just point the Italian wherever you want me." All in all, Dean was a pussycat.

Of course, to put a weekly variety musical on TV every week, there was a factory of behind-the-scenes people such as singers, dancers, choreographers, rehearsal pianists, writers, technicians, and arrangers. Camera set-ups and blockings were done on Saturdays without Dean and the actual shooting schedule was limited to Sundays (with Dean frequently departing the set before the taping was completed!).

The show was often in the Top Ten. In appreciation for the show's success, Dean made a handshake deal with Greg giving him half ownership of the show. The validity of that ownership was the subject of a lawsuit brought by NBC Universal, with judgment going to NBC.

During his lifetime, Greg was nominated for more than a dozen Emmy Awards, although he never won. He died in 2005 of pneumonia at age 81.

While I was on Dean's show, Greg proved his admiration for my work by hiring me to compose and conduct for *The Dom DeLuise Show* (1968 summer replacement for Jackie Gleason); *The 1969 Emmy Awards*; *Gene Kelly's Wonderful World of Girls* (1970); *The Golddiggers Chevy Show* (1971—1972); *The Wacky World of Jonathan Winters* (1972—1973); and the *50th Anniversary NBC Show*.

I guess the industry liked my work on these various specials as I was nominated for three Emmy Awards between 1970 and 1973 for my involvement with *Gene Kelly's Wonderful World of Girls, The Golddiggers Chevy Show,* and *The Wacky World of Jonathan Winters.* Receiving such recognition was quite an honor for me.

One of my favorite comedians that I ever had the pleasure to work with is Dom DeLuise. Not only is Dom a naturally funny man with a sweet soul, he is definitely a man of many talents. He is also a Golden Globe Award nominee, film director, television producer, chef, and author of children's books and of cooking. Outside of *The Dean Martin Show*, Dom is probably best known as a regular in Mel Brooks' outrageous films from the 1970s through the 1990s.

> *"When we were doing the show, Van was just prolific at what he did,"* said Dom DeLuise, age 75. *"After the band played an arrangement that he had written, everyone would cheer. He was just so good at what he did. He's been around a long time and one of my favorite songs of his is 'A-Tisket, A-Tasket.' He was always smiling, and always fun. I always thought to myself when I went into the studio, "Oh, Van's here!" I get very excited when I see him. He's a doll to me. The show was better because of him. He always brought us great music, good fun, and one helluva smile. He's a sophisticated dresser, full of humor and wit. His music comes from his heart. And he's married to the coolest lady for the past 70 years, and that's the very best arrangement of all! I love him."*

Jonathan Winters was also an immensely funny talent. I had known Jonathan a few years earlier from his friendship with Gordon MacRae. When I got to work on Jonathan's show, we got to know each other better. He's so talented and so quick. He was always a threat, meaning he's always on deck to come up with something outrageous. He later became a frequent guest on Dean Martin's *Roasts*.

Despite Dean's reputation as a heavy drinker—a reputation perpetuated via his vanity license plates reading "DRUNKY"—he was remarkably self-disciplined. He was often the first to call it a night, and when not on tour or on a film location liked to go home to be with his wife and children. Shirley MacLaine, in her autobiography, confirmed that Dean was sipping apple juice, not liquor, most of the time onstage. He borrowed the lovable-drunk shtick from Joe E. Lewis, but his convincing portrayals of heavy boozers in *Some Came Running* and Howard Hawks' *Rio Bravo* led to unsubstantiated claims of alcoholism. More often than not, Dean's idea of a good time was playing golf or watching TV, particularly Westerns—not staying with Rat Pack friends Frank Sinatra and Sammy Davis, Jr. into the early hours of the morning.

I can't remember whose talk show it was, but Dean came on with his usual drink in hand and cigarette in his mouth and produced much mirth and laughter with his double-entendre jokes after which the host opened it up for a question-and-answer segment from the audience.

After one or two comical questions, a young teenage girl asked, "Mr. Martin, why don't you join Alcoholics Anonymous?"

Suddenly, a strange quiet came over the audience and Dean quickly departed from his persona, put out his cigarette, stood up and said, "My dear young lady, I do thirty-three TV shows every year. I do at least three major pictures, plus two or three record albums, and appear in Las Vegas and other clubs when I have the time. Now do you think they would pay me this kind of money if I was a drunk?"

The young girl was embarrassed and just said, "Well, I'm sorry. Thank you," and sat down.

Dean was sort of a private person. He didn't want any involvements of any kind. My dear friend Ken Lane, who was Dean's accompanist for nearly 20 years and with Irving Taylor co-wrote "Everybody Loves Somebody" in 1949, once told me, he never had dinner or a one-on-one drink with him. Dean belonged to the Riviera Country Club in Pacific Palisades, California. I never played golf with him but I always wanted to. We spoke about golf very often but he never invited me. I think Dean was about a 12 handicap and he used to play with a bunch of scratch players who would give him strokes. He usually got killed financially when he played but that was the way he wanted it.

Dean very seldom sang a new song or one of the current hits of the day, mainly because he would have to learn the new melodies and the lyrics and he was just more comfortable with songs that he previously recorded or that were old standards.

On one show he was scheduled to sing the familiar "Is It True What They Say About Dixie?" I arranged it in the Bob Crosby style of Dixieland. Dean loved it and suggested we do an album of Dixieland tunes. I was all for it and in 1970 we did his final album for Reprise Records called *Sitting on Top of the World*.

However, the tunes that Dean and producer Jimmy Bowen had selected really didn't lend themselves well to a Dixieland treatment, so the album was sort of a mixture of standard tunes. Dean sang great, but the album never sold well. His vocal renditions of "I Wonder Who's Kissing Her Now" and "Smile" are terrific. I wasn't at the final mixing session and I was unhappy with the orchestra balance that Jimmy supervised.

Another portrayal of Dean's public persona was that of a lady's man. After sliding down a brass poll during the opening of every TV show, Dean would always be surrounded by pretty girls.

In July 1968, as a summer replacement show, *The Golddiggers* premiered with hosts Frank Sinatra, Jr., Joey Heatherton, and Paul Lynde. *The Golddiggers* instantly became a hit. They hosted the next two summer replacement shows for Dean.

During the new season of *The Dean Martin Show*, the girls sang, danced, and performed skits with Dean. The most memorable impression of The Golddiggers was during the 1969-1970 TV season where they surrounded Dean on pillows in a weekly concert spot segment that always started with Dean singing "Welcome to My World."

In 1971, The Golddiggers were so popular that they had their own 30-minute syndicated show with a different male guest star each week. Some of those guests included Van Johnson, Glenn Ford, Doug McClure, Rosey Grier, Buddy Hackett, Dom DeLuise, Steve Allen, John Davidson, Hugh O'Brian, and Martin Milner. Regulars on the show included Larry Storch, Alice Ghostley, Charles Nelson Reilly, Jackie Vernon, Lonnie Shorr, Barbara Heller, Don Rice, and Jennifer Buriner. The Golddiggers as a group was scaled down from twelve to ten and finally went down to eight before disbanding in 1972.

During this period I also arranged and conducted a Christmas album for The Golddiggers called *We Need A Little Christmas* on Metromedia Records, which sold pretty well.

> *"Working with Van was always a pleasure,"* said trumpeter Don Smith, who has played for the Les Brown Band since 1956 and who has played in television and studio recording orchestras led by Van. *"I've worked for a lot of people over the years and I've worked with Van in the studios. Sometimes those situations can be so tense. I won't mention any names, but some people just made such experiences miserable, but with Van it was always a pleasure. He made things so relaxed and pleasant.*
>
> *"There was one situation on The Dean Martin Show where Sid Caesar was the guest. The band does a play on and an underscore (background music while the stars were doing something on camera), and then a playoff for a guest. In those days we worked long hours often doing a dress rehearsal*

followed by the taping of the show on the same day. We were set to play 'Sentimental Journey' as the underscore for Sid Caesar. Butch Stone was the band's librarian and he had removed this particular copy of 'Sentimental Journey' earlier from our order of music. The song was to be played by the Les Brown Band later that night after the taping of the show. When it came time to play the underscore, Les gave the downbeat, and the entire brass section and I played the playoff number very loud instead. We were wrong, of course. It was very embarrassing. We had a meeting of the entire staff orchestra to talk about that. I blamed it on Butch, but to his credit he was always thinking of what he needed to do next. He meant well. I later apologized to Van and he was very nice and understanding about it, saying that things happen. Les didn't say a word. Greg Garrison, the show's producer, wasn't happy about it.

"Van was always cool. The hotter it got, the cooler Van got. That's really a great trait. He was always a gentleman in any situation. Some people would just go off. One leader I worked for, Mitchell Ayers, was the kind of the guy who would go off. He was tough.

"Van would always do something that I thought was funny. He would talk to the band about what he wanted done, and then he would turn to his right and spit. The only thing I could think of where that came from was from his buddy, Butch Stone. It may have been some kind of New York thing, I don't know, but I liked it. It relaxed me, for one thing. I just thought it was kind of funny. I also have to say that, to Van's credit, I've never seen anybody spit that elegantly!"

I considered myself so fortunate to have worked on a successful show with so many talented people. It was not only lucrative for me, but I got the added pleasure of meeting and either arranging or conducting for some of the biggest stars in the entertainment industry. Stars such as Frank Sinatra, The Mills Brothers, Don Cherry, Peggy Lee, Beverly Sills, Louis Armstrong, Leo Durocher, Tommy Tune, Charles Nelson Reilly, Paul Lynde, Joey Heatherton, Frank Sinatra Jr., Vic Damone, Carol Lawrence, Phil Harris…the list is endless.

I have a vivid recollection of one of Bing Crosby's appearances on Dean's show. Our assistant producer/director, Lee Hale, put together a great medley of tunes as a duet between Dean and Bing showing off the super-casual style of the two stars. The taping went well and when it was over, Bing was out the studio door before Dean. He never said goodbye to anyone or said thanks for all the preparation everyone did.

However, earlier in the week, he had asked our rehearsal pianist, Geoff Clarkson, to sketch out a similar medley he could use on the road. Geoff really knocked himself out putting the intricate sketch together even though Bing kept adding tunes and changing the keys after the sketch was finished.

When Geoff finished the project, Bing said he appreciated his work and asked, "Geoff, what do you drink?"

Geoff said, "Oh, really, that's not necessary, Bing."

However, Bing was persistent and finally Geoff said, "Well, Scotch would be OK."

The next day Bing came in and handed Geoff a half-pint bottle of J&B.

I said to Geoff, "What did you say when he handed the small bottle to you?"

Geoff said, "I said, 'Thanks, Bing,'" but I said to myself, 'Now I've got a story to tell the rest of my life.'"

As Lee Hale wrote in his book, *Backstage at the Dean Martin Show*, "Bing Crosby was professional, loose and witty, but he sure flunked generosity."

Lee also related in his book that Phil Harris was a frequent guest on the show, and like Dean, he made a career out of pretending to be the town drunk. They both perfected that image of the glorification of booze.

The writers had an idea for the two of them in which they would engage in a tea party with all the English frills, but the viewing audience would sense that there was something stronger than tea in those cups. Pretty girls in short maid outfits would stroll in and out serving them.

"One lump or two?" Dean asked Phil.

"Dean, you dog. You know I'm driving," Phil quipped in reply.

"Oh my, this is strong tea!" Dean gasped. "I just melted my teaspoon."

None of us were sure just how the J&B got into the teapot but our stage manager said he saw Phil pouring something into it just before the cameras rolled. Sober or not, Phil was a great partner for Dean, and when they were together the cue cards went flying.

I have to say that Lee put his heart and soul into making Dean's show the remarkable success that it was. He was and still is such a talent in creating special material songs and also a genius in putting together video clips for many organizations.

After his book was published, he presented me with an autographed copy, which he inscribed: *To Van — We made beautiful music together — wasn't it great?*

Yes, Lee, it certainly was.

> "Van always reminded me of David Niven—suave, sophisticated, smart and especially good at telling a funny story," said Lee Hale. "He also had good taste in selecting a mate. As for musical abilities, he's the best. We worked together on The Dean Martin Show for many years, and each week's greatest pleasure for me was at the first orchestra rehearsal, when I heard Van's arrangements of what I had outlined earlier. They were always, as he is, very special. Whether he was writing a new score or spinning a new joke, he always made me smile."

Another "shtick" that Dean used on his show that probably originated in his nightclub appearances was his one-line parodies of famous songs. Ken Lane would play an arpeggio leading him and he would sing the following: "Every time it rains, it rains bourbon from Heaven ..." or "Hello, Young Lovers, you're under arrest ..." or "Love walked right in and scared the sh—— adows away ..." The routine always got laughs.

On the last two years of Dean's show, Greg Garrison suddenly realized that he wasn't making any money on the closing theme song, because he wasn't the publisher. All previous years he had used "Everybody Loves Somebody" for the opening and closing themes, which was written by Ken Lane. So Greg asked me to write a new closing theme and, of course, his company, called Barrump-Bump Publishing, would publish the song.

I felt embarrassed about it because Ken would get screwed out of recognition and royalties, so I said to Ken, "Why don't you speak to Dean and tell him what Greg wants to do. After all, your theme is Dean's identification and maybe he can do something about it."

"Are you kidding?" Ken said to me. "Dean would say, 'Fuck it. Don't bother me with these horseshit problems.'"

So Ken never mentioned it to Dean. I went ahead and wrote the closing theme and called it "A Whole Lot of Lovin'" and Lee Hale wrote the lyrics so that The Golddiggers could use it. Barrump-Bump Music published it. Greg made some money as I did, too, as ASCAP logged every performance. I also conducted an album for Barrump-Bump Records of various popular television themes called *T.V. Themes by Van Alexander and his Orchestra.*

As the 1974 television season drew to a close, *The Dean Martin Show* had eight terrific years on the air with great Nielson ratings, but we had a decline in viewing of late and Greg and the staff were concerned. Maybe the viewing audience was getting tired and blasé about musical variety shows.

Luckily, we had choreographer Ed Kerrigan and our right-arm, Lee Hale, who hit upon the idea of "toasting" a different guest star each week. Greg liked the word "toast," but it reminded him of the word "roast" and he said, "Let's do it like a Friar's Club roast, and have some good fun spoofing famous stars."

He added, "It doesn't have to be musical; in fact, it'll be better without it."

Greg was never really music conscious, as he hated the musicians union.

So that was the beginning of a whole new concept for Dean and the show. Dean loved it. He didn't have to sing or learn new songs, nor did he have to rehearse. *The Dean Martin Celebrity Roast* lasted for two more years on TV and would later appear as television specials.

The roast turned out to be very successful, albeit it didn't do any good for Les Brown and his band and for me as arranger. But it was great for Greg, Dean, Lee Hale, and others. It was easy to book guest stars as everyone was anxious to be roasted on *The Dean Martin Celebrity Roast.* The list of people who were roasted included Johnny Carson, Carroll O'Connor, Don Rickles, Senator Hubert Humphrey, Joe Namath, Hank Aaron, Redd Foxx, Rowan and Martin, Senator Barry Goldwater, then-governor Ronald Reagan, Bob Hope, Jack Benny, Jimmy Stewart, the Rev. Billy Graham, Jackie Gleason, and Lucille Ball, among others. *Roast* regulars who gave testimonials included Foster Brooks, who played an inebriated character who would claim some sort of association with the guest of honor, Red Buttons, Nipsey Russell, Dan Rowan and Dick Martin, and Shelia MacRae.

During the early 1980s, Dean spent some of his time appearing in concert with Frank Sinatra and Sammy Davis Jr., reprising their Rat Pack years.

Dean's world began to crumble on March 21, 1987, when his son Dean Paul was killed when his jet fighter crashed while flying with the Air National Guard. In addition to never completely recovering from losing his son, Dean suffered from emphysema. He unofficially retired from performing soon afterwards. For the most part, he became a recluse.

In the late fall of 1995, Beth and I were having dinner at Da Vinci's in Beverly Hills. I saw Dean sitting in a booth all by himself. He needed a shave and had his teeth in a glass. He looked awful.

Before we left the restaurant, I went over to Dean and said hello and tried to make small talk with him like, "Have you seen Ken Lane and how is he doing?"

"Yeah, I spoke to him, but he's still drinking," Dean said in a rather lethargic voice.

That was the last time I saw or spoke to dear old Dino. He passed away a short time later of acute respiratory failure at his home in Beverly Hills on Christmas morning 1995, at age 78.

I was profoundly saddened to hear the news. Dean was a talented entertainer and comic genius who was always very pleasant with me even though we were never close friends. He left a legacy in entertainment history with his marvelous recordings, critically acclaimed movies, and, of course, his hilarious television shows.

I was also saddened to hear a few months later of the passing of Ken Lane, who died of emphysema in Lake Tahoe, California. He was 84.

After *The Dean Martin Show* folded, I decided to take life a little easier, spend more time with my family and try to lower my golf handicap. After almost forty years of nonstop years in music, I felt that the time had come to stop and smell the roses.

Working with my boss and good friend Gordon MacRae on a recording project at Capitol Records. Working as Gordon's musical director for ten years was a delight as we recorded thirteen albums together and performed at all the top spots throughout the world. God, I miss him.

Guy Mitchell and I ready to play golf in 1970 in Las Vegas. For years after *The Guy Mitchell Show* ended, Guy and I remained close friends until his death in 1999.

Above: Dean Martin and I got together for this photo after one of the tapings of *The Dean Martin Show.* I had eight wonderful years working as assistant musical director for the show. Dean was a pussycat, although we never got to be real close friends.

Below: A photo taken off the television screen of my credit for conducting music for that particular episode of *The Dean Martin Show.*

Above: It was always great to get together with my good friend Les Brown. I had a wonderful association with him both personally and professionally for over 60 years. I miss him.

Below: Here I am pictured with Les Brown, Corky Hale, and ace arranger and composer Pete Rugolo.

Above: Good friends Bea Wain and Kay Starr were there in 2005 to help me celebrate my 90th birthday.

Below: Me and the *other* Ray Charles at the Big Band Academy of America's Annual Reunion.

Left: I was proud to shake drummer extraordinaire Louis Bellson's hand upon his receiving The Golden Bandstand Award from the Big Band Academy of America in March 2005.

Below: Having this autographed photo of Louis Armstrong is one of my most treasured possessions. Satchmo inscribed: "To Van Alexander: The Real Man of Music." Wow! I was floored.

LOUIS ARMSTRONG
And His Famous Orchestra

Personal Management
JOE GLASER
R C A Building 30 Rockefeller Plaza
New York N. Y

Getting together with Dom DeLuise and Lee Hale from *The Dean Martin Show.*

Left: Shaking hands with Bob Hope after I received the Irwin Kostal Award from ASMAC in 1995.

Above: Here I am in 1995 receiving the Irwin Kostal Award from ASMAC pictured with me are (l-r) Irwin Kostal, Jr., Stan Freberg, and Larry Blank.

Below: Billy May and Bob Hope joined me for a photo op at the 1995 ASMAC Awards. Billy was presented The Golden Score Award that evening. What a marvelous talent he was!

While on *The Dean Martin Show*, I had the privilege of working with a variety of talented guest stars. None came any finer than Peggy Lee (shown left) going over a score with me in 1971, and with Beverly Sills (below).

Left: Here I am recently with my former student and dear friend Johnny Mandel. What a success story Johnny is!

Visiting a few years ago at the Big Band Academy of America's Annual Reunion with good friends Benny Carter and his wife Hilma. Benny's music was astounding and way ahead of its time. We all miss Benny and his music.

Above: I am enjoying a light-hearted moment with some of my colleagues in the business: (L to R) Ian Fraser, Lennie Neihaus, Spud Murphy, and Bob Florence. Sadly, Spud and Bob are no longer with us to help create beautiful music.

Below: Chatting with trombonist Herbie Harper and arranger/composer Frank Comstock in 2002 at Butch Stone's 90th Birthday Bash at the Sportsmen Lodge in Studio City.

Here I am posed in a group photo in 1963 with the CBS Composers. Back Row: Morton Stevens, George Duning; Middle Row: Cyril Mockridge, Muzzy Marcellino, Wilbur Hatch, Richard Shores, Nelson Riddle, Curt Massey, Harry Sukman, me, John Parker, Nathan Scott, Jack Pleis, Perry Botkin, Harry Zimmerman, Paul Weston. Front Row: Harry Geller, Jeff Alexander, Lalo Schifrin, Perry Lafferty, Leon Klatzkin, and Richard Markowitz.

Beth and I were on hand to help celebrate Max and Ida Herman's 60th wedding anniversary. Max served over 30 years as president of Local 47.

Here I am pictured with the late Milt Bernhart, who was a West Coast Jazz icon and former president of the Big Band Academy of America.

CHAPTER NINE
GIVE ME THE SIMPLE LIFE

Since I was now officially in semi-retirement, I allowed myself to do occasional freelance work only if the project appealed to me and if it didn't involve all-night deadlines. I also wanted to stay connected to the music business by being a part of various music industry organizations such as ASCAP, ASMAC, and The Big Band Academy of America, among others.

After taking a long-overdue Caribbean cruise in July 1982, with Beth and her older sister Carolyn Schiff, we disembarked in Miami and flew up to New York City and prepared ourselves for a very exciting experience. I had received an invitation, along with other arrangers-conductors, to be a guest conductor for one performance at the famous Radio City Music Hall. It was a celebration of the 50th anniversary of the building of this marvelous music hall. It was a thrill for me to be asked to conduct the Radio City Music Hall Orchestra. As a youngster, I had spent many hours enjoying the opulence and listening to the superb orchestra as I excitedly watched them rise from the pit to above the stage. There was to be no payment involved and no funds provided for airfare for this event, but I didn't care. I was going to rise from the pit. I was given a dozen or so tickets for friends and relatives. My brother David and his wife Lila came; as did my cousins Janet and Stan Kane, Bernice Katz, and Sis and Bernie Cohen; and my old friend Dick Raymond. So, I felt well represented.

Robert Jani was in charge of the Golden Anniversary Celebration. He had sent me a score and an audiocassette of the music I would be conducting. Since there would be no time for individual rehearsal, this would allow me to become familiar with the score. It was a medley of well-known overtures: "William Tell," "Romeo and Juliet," and concluding with a rousing rendition of the "1812 Overture" (minus the canons, of course!).

My guests were all seated in the first row mezzanine. Mr. Jani informed me that I would be introduced and be on the podium of the rising pit right after intermission. I couldn't wait. I was really excited. He suggested that I sit with him in the orchestra section and watch the first part of the show.

There are 6,500 seats in this theater and would you believe that I sat on the one seat that had a large wad of chewing gum on it! I was wearing my tuxedo and I was going to rise from the pit with bubble gum on my ass. Mr. Jani rushed me backstage and called a wardrobe lady who gently iced the rear end of my trousers and rubbed it with cleaning fluid finishing just in time for me to go down into the pit and get onto the podium so I could make my rise with dignity. What a trauma!

The orchestra was wonderful. They followed my tempos, and afterward, we all had a good laugh. However, I realized again that nostalgia isn't what it used to be. The beautiful lobby of Radio City Music Hall was now a hustle bustle of vendors selling T-shirts and souvenirs and hot dogs and pretzels. I guess you really can't ever go home again. It's probably better to remember certain things as they were.

After the show, I hosted a late supper party for my guests. So, in spite of the chewing gum incident, the T-shirt and food vendors, and the general dirtiness outside, it was a thrill of a lifetime for me and I'm so glad I took the opportunity to do it.

In 1989, I collaborated once again with the great Lalo Schifrin on a two-hour television movie called *The Neon Empire*, about the New York Jewish mob building the first Las Vegas casino, starring Ray Sharkey, Gary Busey, and Martin Landau.

I first worked with Lalo in late 1966 when he asked me to write a few cues for the movie *Cool Hand Luke*, starring Paul Newman. Lalo was the film's composer. We had developed a very nice rapport and years later he became the conductor of the Glendale (California) Symphony Orchestra. He called me saying that he was going to do some summer "Pops" concerts. One of themes of these concerts was going to be music of the 1940s. He asked if I could write a symphonic arrangement of "A-Tisket, A-Tasket." I was more than happy to do it. It was a bit of a challenge, but it turned out so well that he asked me to write a few more arrangements of that era: "Opus One," "King Porter Stomp," and the ever-popular "When The Saints Go Marching In," among others. My wonderful and valued association with Lalo continues today.

On May 29, 1992, the University of Southern California proposed to give a "seventy-something" birthday bash for Ella Fitzgerald. Six weeks prior to the event, their planning committee called me asking me if they might use my name on the honorary dinner committee. They told me there would be no obligation of any kind on my part. Because of my past association with Ella, I told them that I would be honored.

A few days later, they called me again. They asked if I would help them get a group of all-star musicians together, those of whom Ella knew and with whom she would feel comfortable, in case she wanted to get up and sing a few numbers; their ultimate goal. The entire evening would be to benefit the USC School of Music, as the committee was planning to establish a scholarship in Ella's name.

After making many, many telephone calls, I succeeded in securing the "gratis" services of the following group of musicians: Louie Bellson, drums; Marshall Royal, alto sax; Buddy Collette, tenor sax; Snooky Young, trumpet; Gerald Wiggins, piano; and Dave Stone, bass. Not a bad conclave of all-star musicians. I also had confirmed commitments from two great singers: Joe Williams and Herb Jeffries.

I remembered that I had arranged an old tune for Chick Webb years ago that was sung by trumpeter Taft Jordan. The song was called "Ella." I thought this song would be perfect for the occasion. I wrote out a new lead sheet, updating it a bit, and I added a second chorus with new lyrics. I played it for the planning committee and they loved it. They suggested that Herb Jeffries sing it. However, Dean Livingston of USC thought that I should sing it to Ella, just like I had done for the planning committee. He felt that Ella would be thrilled and that the song would mean so much more to her coming from me. I, of course, agreed to do it. So, what began as just using my name on the dinner committee now had me involved in booking the all-star band, arranging a song and singing a song in the show. But, wait...there's more...

During the early stages of planning for this affair, Steve Allen was asked to write a tribute song dedicated to Ella, which he said he would love to do. Four days before the event, no one had heard from Steve. His song then finally arrived. It was a lovely song called "When Ella Sings." I quickly set up a rehearsal with Herb Jeffries, who had agreed to perform it. We met at my home and I made a cassette tape in his key for him to take home to rehearse. He loved the song. Okay, everything seemed to be working well; everything was in order, right? Wrong!

It is now the evening of the affair. Everyone is there looking elegant in their formal attire. In comes Herb Jeffries with his lovely wife Regina. Herb walks over to me and whispers that he can't talk. He lost his voice due to a bad case of laryngitis. He wasn't kidding either. He really could not talk above a whisper.

The Steve Allen song was on the program and the committee was in a panic. What to do? What to do? Dean Livingston suggested that I sing the song. After rehearsing it so many times, I did know the song. Because of the predicament we found ourselves in, I agreed to do the song. I practically became the producer and the star of the show.

The evening was a huge success. The all-star band was just that. The star-studded audience appeared to have liked my two numbers and they went wild when Ella got up to sing a few songs alone and then a few with the incomparable Joe Williams. Dean Livingston and the entire committee were so appreciative of my contributions that for days afterwards, they continued to call and write beautiful notes, all of which I have kept in my "I Get Letters" file.

Nineteen ninety-five was a real banner year for my ego and career. I am a past president of the American Society of Music Arrangers and Composers (ASMAC), having served in that capacity from 1986 to 1988. First organized in 1938, ASMAC is an organization whose mission is to promote the arts of Music Arranging, Composition and Orchestration within the entertainment industry community and the general public. Each year ASMAC holds a black-tie event in which it honors certain arrangers/composers for their accomplishments over the years. That year the Board of Directors voted to honor Billy May and me. Billy received the Golden Score Award. I was the first recipient of the Irwin Kostal Award, named after Irwin Kostal, the late Academy Award–winning composer renown for his work in television and in such classic films as *West Side Story* and *The Sound of Music*, and a former president of ASMAC. The plaque read: "For consistent achievement in music arranging, orchestration, and composition."

The award was presented to me on September 15, 1995, at the Universal Hilton Hotel. My entire family as well as many friends and colleagues, including Bob and Dolores Hope, attended the gala evening. It was a proud night for me.

Larry Blank, the renowned Broadway and musical theater composer and arranger as well as a former president of ASMAC, presented me with this coveted award.

"Van is really the teacher of us all," said Larry Blank. *"He taught me about how to give back by using the talent one has. About the same time as the ASMAC Awards are given there is an event called 'The Share Show.' The Hollywood wives, many of whom are performers, put on this fundraiser show every year for under-privileged children. The arrangers always donated their services. The show always had very big stars. Hank Mancini used to write for it. Van was always part of the show and he pushed me into it as well. I remember him telling me very distinctly, 'Write what you know how to write and it will sound great.' Plus, Van's gift of humor can always quell a tense situation."*

One of the finer musicians I've gotten to know through my association with ASMAC is John Clayton, the Grammy Award-winning bassist, composer and conductor. John is a well-respected name in the music business and jazz enthusiasts more readily know him as the founder of the Clayton-Hamilton Jazz Orchestra with his saxophonist brother Jeff Clayton and drummer Jeff Hamilton. John is the current president of ASMAC.

"Van Alexander exemplifies 'The Walk,'" said John Clayton. *"Van doesn't just talk the talk; he walks the walk. Just listen to his music! He represents a loving, gentlemanly way of being and his approach to life (just take his often-used line when introducing his wife: 'You remember my first wife, Beth?'). His music, his lifestyle, his friends and colleagues all define what Van is to me: The classiest act on earth."*

Another talented gentleman that I've become friends with through my affiliation with ASMAC is Ray Charles. Ray self-deprecatingly bills himself as "the *other* Ray Charles" in a humorous tribute to the late blues singer with whom he worked on several occasions. Ray, a two-time Emmy Award winner, is best known as the organizer and leader of The Ray Charles Singers who were featured on Perry Como's records, radio shows and television shows for 35 years, and who were also known for a series of 30 choral record albums produced in the 1950s and 1960s. As a vocalist, Ray, along with Julia Rinker Miller, is known for singing the theme song to the television series *Three's Company*, starring John Ritter ("Come and Knock On Our Door").

> *"Van is a wonderful, well-dressed man and a real gentleman,"* said Ray Charles, age 90. *"I've known of Van for many years but I didn't meet him until about 20 years ago through our association as board members of ASMAC. It was an honor to serve on the board with him because Van's strength lies in his pragmatism. He thinks straight about musicians' problems. He's very aware of them. He's very practical in his approach to things. He's very kind. He looks out for people."*

In May 1996, the Pacific Pioneer Broadcasters honored me at a luncheon at the Sportsmen's Lodge in Sherman Oaks with their Diamond Circle Award. I was honored for having made an important contribution to the development of broadcasting and being age 75 or older—hence, the award named Diamond. The plaque was inscribed: "For many distinguished years in radio and television."

A few weeks later, I received a proclamation from the City of Los Angeles signed by then-Mayor Richard Riordan and the entire City Council.

In March 1997, I was presented the Golden Bandstand Award by the Big Band Academy of America. This fine organization, to preserve and support Big Band music, was started by Leo Walker in the 1980s, and was later presided over by West Coast jazz icon Milt Bernhart. Milt did an incredible job at the BBAA's helm until his untimely death in 2004. In recent years I served as this organization's vice-president. Since Milt's passing, his son, David, has charted the organization through some choppy waters as membership has decreased over the past few years.

Also in that same year, the Los Angeles Jazz Society honored me with its Composer-Arranger Award.

On April 30, 2002, the American Society of Composers, Arrangers and Publishers (ASCAP) presented me with its Lifetime Achievement Award. ASCAP is a non-profit performance rights organization that protects its members' musical copyrights by monitoring public performances of their music, whether via a broadcast or live performance, and compensating them accordingly. I've been a member of ASCAP since 1941.

I also got to work commercially on an album one last time with my dear friend Les Brown. Just prior to his passing away in January 2001, he asked me to write an arrangement of "Ain't She Sweet" for his new album, *Session # 55*. I was more than happy to do it. It would be Les' final album as a bandleader. Les, Jr., who has since assumed leadership of his dad's Band of Renown which is now based in Branson, Missouri, produced the album.

> *"Musically, Van is a giant,"* said Les Brown, Jr. *"Van is always a dapper gentleman. He's a classy guy. Above and beyond that, he is one of the all-time great swing arrangers. On our Session # 55 album what I appreciated more than anything was the timelessness of Van's arranging and his concepts. He wrote the arrangement to 'Ain't She Sweet' which we do all the time. When you listen to that piece you hear all those elements and it goes back to the 1930s when he was writing. Going into 2001, he was still able to write in swing and to make it timely and sound good by today's standards. That's remarkable.*
>
> *"I first worked with Van professionally while producing an album my dad did for His Majesty King Bhumibol Adulyadej of Thailand. His Majesty is a huge jazz fan as well as a saxophonist and he commissioned the Les Brown Band to make a private album of songs that he had written commemorating either the 20th or 30th year of his reign. The band recorded the material. It's a remarkably beautiful package that was never for commercial sale. Van worked on a few arrangements on that album.*
>
> *"Van and my dad were very close. My parents, along with Van and Beth, celebrated the same anniversary date. He's always been close with my family and I'm very fond of him. His genuine friendliness and attitude always impressed me. We tend to see musicians in a different light. Van has always been a very classy, honest man with incredible integrity. He's always very helpful, encouraging, and understanding. He's also a great teacher. A lot of guys have studied arranging with Van through the years. His warmth probably strikes me more than anything.*
>
> *"Musicians to this day talk about the Dean Martin television show and I'm always amazed at how many people come up to me and know of two arrangers: Van Alexander and Jay Hill. It always surprises me that people would go into that*

much research to find out who did all that writing. Van is an unsung hero."

Another close personal and professional association I have had through the Les Brown Band came by way of Les' kid brother, Clyde "Stumpy" Brown, who played trombone and sang novelty tunes in the Band of Renown since 1944. Now at age 83, Stumpy has since retired from the music business.

> *"Besides being a fine arranger and a great musician, Van was always a gentleman,"* said Stumpy Brown. *"He's one of the nicest gentlemen you'll ever want to meet. I first met Van in 1940, when I was attending the New York Military Academy. He came up there with his band to play for a dance. He always had a pretty good band. I was 15 at the time. (Johnny Mandel was a year behind me.) Later on, I did record dates for Van. I worked with him on a number of television shows, including The Dean Martin Show, and on movie calls. He's always a gentleman."*

Semi-retirement has also allowed me to reconnect more meaningfully with many of my wonderful friends I've made throughout the years in this business. One who immediately comes to mind is Patty Andrews, known as "the girl in the middle" of the fabulous hit-making singing trio, The Andrews Sisters. I've known Patty for years. She and her husband, Walt Weschler, now live in retirement and Beth and I get together with them frequently for dinner engagements.

> *"Van is such a beautiful person,"* said Patty Andrews-Weschler, age 90. *"He wrote all my orchestrations when I did my solo act. He's such a wonderful arranger. He did such a fantastic job. I consider him a very dear and close friend."*

Another close friend is trumpeter Rubin "Zeke" Zarchy, who in his younger days couldn't hold down a job if his life depended on it! All kidding aside, Zeke was a marvelous lead trumpeter who played in the bands of Benny Goodman, Bob Crosby, Artie Shaw, Red Norvo, Tommy Dorsey, and in both Glenn Miller's civilian and military outfits. At age

93, Zeke is not in the best of health these days and when I asked him if he would be kind of enough to offer a quote for this book, Zeke wrote: *"Van Alexander, one of the best musically and otherwise."* Thanks, Zeke, what you wrote means a lot to me.

Still another gifted lead trumpet player that is a dear friend of mine is Max Herman, who was the bedrock in the Bob Crosby band until 1942. Max's musical impact was most profoundly felt for decades while serving as the President of the Musicians' Union Local 47 in Los Angeles. Max holds the distinct title of President Emeritus of Musicians' Union Local 47 and Executive Board Member Emeritus of the American Federation of Musicians.

> *"I have known Van since way back in 1936. He was a giant in those days as he was a giant his whole life,"* said Max Herman, age 94. *"I don't know anybody who has done more to build the Big Bands than he has. Many of the outstanding musicians with whom I've worked with over the years got their start with Van Alexander. Van was always one of my big supporters when I presided over Local 47. He knew my background. He knew I represented the musicians. That's why they kept me in that position for 30 years.*
>
> *"Van Alexander is a talented composer/conductor and bandleader/arranger and one of the Patriarch Fathers of the glorious Big Band era. The Big Band Academy of America would not be alive if it weren't for him because Van is a pro."*

Anytime I have a chance to pal around with Bea Wain, it's always a treat. She's charming, witty, funny, and always stimulating. I'm sure you all remember Bea. She helped Larry Clinton to score a batch of hit recordings such as "My Reverie" and "Deep Purple" while garnering Best Female Band Vocalist honors in a 1939 *Billboard* magazine poll.

> *"Van is one of the dearest, nicest gentlemen that I have ever met,"* said Bea Wain, age 91. *"He's a rare guy. I love him. Obviously, he's a fine musician. When my late husband, André Baruch, and I moved out to Los Angeles in 1980, I became friendly with Van more than I had back East. Of*

course, I have always admired his work. André and Van played golf together. Both were good golfers and enjoyed each other's company.

"On several occasions Van did some arrangements for me for some Big Bands shows of which I was involved. There was a particular song that I wanted to sing and I didn't have the chart and Van came through and wrote it beautifully. I've also watched him conduct many times, of course. We are more social friends than professional friends. Even to this day, very often he, Beth and I would go out to dinner. It's always a joy."

Then there are the wonderful associations I continue to have today with fellow colleagues such as Sammy Nestico, Frank Comstock and John Williams. Sammy's mark is that of a prolific composer and arranger of Big Band music. Sammy is most known for his arrangements for the Count Basie orchestra. Leading symphonies have also played his arrangements, but he is most proud of the nearly 600 numbers published in the education field and played in schools throughout America.

"When I came to town with no friends here, Van was eager and willing to help me," said Sammy Nestico, age 88. *"In a city where everyone seems to be protecting their jobs and are reluctant to help a newcomer in their field, I felt this spoke mountains about Van Alexander. Knowing Van has been one of the personal and musical highlights of my career. He brings an uncommon dignity to an industry where it is never in long supply. A quiet, gentle man, he is a person who understands the spirit, the meaning and beauty of music. His manner earns him the respect of his peers. Being in his presence has always been a pleasure. I had always hoped that some of those qualities would 'rub off' on me. I love the guy."*

Frank Comstock was just 20 years old when his smooth swinging arrangements caught the ear of bandleader Les Brown who hired him on the spot. In addition, Frank has written for the Rocky and Bullwinkle cartoons, Jack Webb's *Pete Kelly's Blues* and for Webb's *Dragnet* television series as well as for many other TV shows, including *McHale's Navy, Happy Days, Laverne and Shirley,* and *Adam-12.*

"I've known Van for so many years that I think of him as my ol' pal," said Frank Comstock, age 90. *"I never think of him as an arranger or anything like that. I just think of him as a nice man, somebody that I've known and liked for years.*

"Van would periodically write out special novelty tunes for his pal Butch Stone to sing when Butch was in the Les Brown band. This one particular time Les asked me to write out a novelty tune for Butch called 'Tris-Ca-Deck-A-Phobia' (about the fear of the Number 13). I did so and the next time I saw Van I asked how come he didn't do that tune. He said, 'I don't even know how to spell it!' We had a good laugh about that it.

"I once kiddingly told him that I learned all my arranging from him as he's about 10 years older than me. But in reality, I learned most of my stuff from listening to the Jimmie Lunceford band. Van and I are good friends. I like his work; he likes my work."

The name John Williams is synonymous with musical Americana. A five-time Academy Award winner and ten-time Grammy Award recipient, John is recognized for composing theme music for four Olympic Games as well as having composed many of the most famous film scores in history including *Star Wars, E.T., Superman, Harry Potter,* and all four of the *Indiana Jones* projects.

I first met John Williams in the early 1960s when I was scoring a few pictures at Columbia. John was playing piano in the studio orchestra. During the early 1980s the major studios were promoting their pictures before Academy Award time by giving lavish cocktail and dinner parties to solicit support for their films. This particular night we were dining at 20th Century-Fox and after a couple of drinks John Williams walked by my table, slapped me on the back and said, "Hey, Jeff, how the hell are ya?" (Jeff Alexander was a friend and fellow arranger/composer.) I quickly corrected him saying, "No, John, I'm not Jeff. I'm Van."

Well, he apologized and two days later I received this note: "Dear Van—Cannot forgive myself for calling you 'Jeff' last night!! From now on you have my full permission to call me 'Cootie.' Best, John." (For you younger readers, Cootie Williams was a marvelous trumpet player who was a stalwart with Duke Ellington for decades.)

I was pretty much resting on my professional laurels, so to speak, not doing much writing at all when my friend, four-time Grammy Award nominee Michael Feinstein, called me in 2004 asking me to do some work for his upcoming Carnegie Hall concert debut. Michael's invitation got me back into much appreciated action.

"Van is a musical survivor," said Michael Feinstein, age 52. *"He transcended many different eras of music and created beautiful sounds for multiple generations and has lived to tell the tale. Van has a unique point of view on the music we did for my Carnegie Hall concert. When I decided to do a Benny Goodman tribute, there were any number of people I could have asked to create the arrangement. But Van was there. I wanted somebody to do it who lived the era so it would be an organic experience. It would not be copying an earlier style, but it was Van just dipping back into that part of his life. It wasn't something that he read in a book or studied how to do. He lived it. He knew exactly how to create those sounds. That was unique to him. There was nobody else around who was alive from that era who was still active and able to do that. I was already familiar with Van's work having worked with him a few years earlier. He did an arrangement that I ultimately didn't record but I have used: 'This Love of Mine.'*

"Whenever I meet a musician whose work that I admire, especially if they are an arranger, I'll ask if we can work together, if we can do something together. I met Van at an ASMAC event and asked him if he would an arrangement for me. He was very sweet and said yes. And he did "This Love of Mine." I knew his work from the Big Band Era, and, of course, I knew 'A-Tisket, A-Tasket.' I also knew his name from the seeming endless and infinite number of recordings he had done during his time with Capitol Records, the Sigmund Romberg operetta recordings he had done of The Desert Song and The Student Prince, and the rearrangements he had done of those classic scores which are marvelous adaptations because they are true to the harmonic intent of Romberg but they also have an extra little energy to them that makes them distinctive and unique presentations of the Romberg material. There are so many re-

cordings that Van's name appears on. He was a busy, busy guy. His name has just been ubiquitous. I also have different radio broadcasts he is on, particularly with Gordon MacRae. I was always impressed by the scope of what he was able to do. He is a rare bird in that he has a distinctive sound, but he also, I think, in many ways, is more versatile than your average arranger in that he had so many different assignments throughout his career that he is able to create a multiplicity of different styles, so much so that it would be easy for the uninitiated to not be able to recognize that he does have a distinctive sound.

"Van is a very sweet, beautiful soul. He's a very lovely man who is highly admired by others, by his associates. I think it is his positive outlook on life that has sustained him for so many years, being an elder statesman. I think that longevity is something as to how one lives their life and I think the fact that he lives a very happy existence in spite of the fact that many people when they get to that age are not so comfortable, especially when physical problems occur. He clearly has taken a view of life that has given him energy and joy. It has sustained him and has kept him alive. I think that it is an object lesson in how to live. I have admiration for him on that level in addition to his extraordinary musical talents."

Wow! I'm humbled by such accolades. I'm always touched by the admiration expressed to me from my peers. It makes my head swell at times.

One becomes more aware of one's own mortality when close friends and colleagues pass on. Such wonderful and talented artists who have "taken a cab" during the writing of this book include Bill Finegan, Bob Florence, Earle Hagen, Jo Stafford, Connie Haines, Neal Hefti, Louis Bellson, Dom DeLuise, and my dear and close friend, Butch Stone. They will be missed. Thankfully, they all left their mark in music that will be felt for generations. They will be missed. Thankfully, they all left their mark in music that will be felt for generations.

Throughout my career, I have been more than blessed to work with a *Who's Who* of talented artists. However, there are some artists with whom I never had the opportunity of working. My "Wish List" would have included Rosemary Clooney, Perry Como, Fred Astaire, Nat "King" Cole, Tony Martin, and Duke Ellington.

To top it all off as being a musical relic, I will finally have the opportunity of being housed in a museum. That's right. In December 2008, I was interviewed and filmed by representatives from the Smithsonian Institute in Washington, D.C., to be added to their jazz archives collection about Chick Webb and Ella. That's an honor in and of itself. With that bit of historical documentation, I suppose you can say that I have come full circle in my career.

I started off as an arranger, then composer, and then bandleader. If I had made any contribution to the world of music, I hope it was to bring credibility, respect, and importance to the task of helping to make a piece of music sound like it has a life of its own. As I have always said, and please excuse me as I repeat myself once again: An arranger is a composer's best friend.

Being an arranger, I'm reminded of this joke about arrangers: A woman walks into a pet store wanting to buy a songbird. While looking around she hears this bird singing beautifully. As if in a trance, she follows the sound of the song. There in the cage is a cheerful songbird singing its little heart out. A sign reads, "One thousand dollars for the pair." She looked deeper in the cage and way in the back she saw this other really haggard-looking and obviously exhausted bird with his head down, shaking his head left to right.

The clerk came over and the woman said, "How much is it just for the songbird that's singing?"

The clerk said, "I'm sorry, you'll have to buy the pair."

The woman said, "But that other bird looks sick and haggard and shaking his head while the other bird is so happy and singing beautifully. Why do I have to buy the other bird?"

The clerk took one beat and said, "Because he's his arranger."

While all such attention and praise from my peers is wonderful to receive, I have to say in all honesty, getting to reconnect with my family during this period had profound blessings for me.

One of the ways I reconnected with Beth and the girls was spending time going on vacations together and traveling.

In December of 1982, Beth and I decided to surprise our entire family (eleven strong) and take them on a cruise to the Caribbean. It was such a wonderful trip that it was the first of three cruises that we took with them all. The second one was to Alaska to see the mighty ice-blue glaciers. We went salmon fishing and caught quite a few. We brought them back to the ship and the chef prepared them for our dinner. We never tasted anything so delicious!

The next cruise was back to the Caribbean, going through the Panama Canal. This was a Christmas cruise. Tragically, just before this trip, Harvey Harris, Joyce's husband, had lost his son Gregory to cancer. Harvey, understandably, decided not to join us. He insisted that Joyce go with us. So, at the last minute, she said she would come with us. Joyce stayed in the cabin with Carolyn Schiff, Beth's older sister. As always, we had a wonderful trip.

Beth, Carolyn and I had a few terrific trips by ourselves. We returned for another visit to Alaska. We had a marvelous cruise to the Scandinavian countries. We flew to Hamburg, West Germany, where we boarded the *Vistaford* and cruised to Oslo, Helsinki, Copenhagen, and Stockholm.

On September 22, 1988, Beth and I celebrated our 50th Golden wedding anniversary. Our two lovely daughters, Joyce and Lynn, along with their two lovely husbands, Harvey and Bob, hosted a marvelous party for us at the fashionable Chasen's Restaurant. It was quite an affair. All of our family and friends were there. David and Lila flew in for the occasion from the East. All four of our grandchildren spoke and gave us a toast.

In 1993, Joyce and Harv, Lynn and Bob, and Beth and I took a marvelous cruise to the Greek Islands. We cruised on the beautiful *Radisson*. We began our journey in Rome and then toured all the wonderful islands that included the ancient Greek ruins, the Acropolis and the Parthenon. We had only one slight mishap. It seems that Joyce and Harv thought it would be fun to rent a motorbike and ride around the island of Santorini. The walking tour was fine for the remaining four of us. Joyce and Harv took a fall, skidding on some gravel and had to be taken back to the ship in sickbay to repair their wounds. They were banged up pretty good. I consoled them, I think, when I told them there was a Jewish word for them..."Schmucks." They recovered and the rest of trip was perfect.

When Joyce married Harv, Beth and I were concerned. Harv was 18 years older than Joyce. However, he was such a wonderful person and so loving to Joyce. After sharing 25 years of marriage together, Harv suddenly suffered a stroke on November 22, 2004, and passed away. He was like a son to me—very warm and generous

Upon returning home from our Greek Islands cruise, things at our house in Encino started to disintegrate. The house was pretty old now, the pipes were rusty, and were in dire need of replacement. Some of our beautiful giant pine trees in the yard were diseased and had to be cut down. The house had served its purpose; it was time to move on. We decided to sell.

We sold the house in ten days. With Lynn and Joyce's love and devotion, we found a great condo on the fashionable Wilshire Boulevard. Bonnie Green, the widow of Johnny Green, an old friend and musical colleague of mine, had previously owned it. It seemed just right. Lynn and Joyce worked like beavers to get the place decorated and ready for us. Moving out of a home after 28 years of residency is a horrendous job. But we got through it and in early November 1994, we moved in. We love it here and we enjoy every day.

In May 1995, a wonderful party was thrown for me on the occasion of my 80th birthday. It was given at the very swank Armani Restaurant in Beverly Hills. It was a beautiful party with toasts and roasts from all and even Lynn and Joyce did their famous rendition of "Sisters," from the movie *White Christmas*.

In September 1996, Beth and I celebrated our 58th wedding anniversary by embarking on a nine-day cruise down the California Coast. We spent two days in San Francisco and the remaining time on the beautiful *Seaborne Pride* trekking the Pacific Ocean along the Golden State. The first Port of Call was Monterey where I played 18 holes at the marvelous Poppy Hill Golf Course. This is one of the courses used in the famous Bing Crosby Pebble Beach Tournament. It was a wonderful trip, a wonderful memory.

It was during these early semi-retirement years—in 1980 to be exact—that my mother was diagnosed with cancer and passed away peacefully. It was a terrible blow for me as I was very close to my mother. Her love and devotion grounded me and I was forever grateful to her for giving me the gift of music. Beth and I went back East for her funeral. She is buried with my father and grandparents in New Jersey.

Four years later, I got the scare of my life. I was diagnosed with colon cancer. It was detected during a routine physical. All sorts of dreaded thoughts filtered through my mind after hearing the news. Luckily, the doctors detected it early and I didn't require chemotherapy or radiation treatments. But I had the colon removed and it was necessary for me to wear the dreaded "pouch." At first it was a devastating blow, but I slowly learned to cope and in a short time I was living a normal life. Yes, I could go swimming, eat and drink most anything I wanted and even resumed a fairly normal sex life. So I'm again so grateful for my complete recovery and would counsel anyone with a similar condition not to despair but rather to be grateful that you can survive and go on with your life.

Now, if you'll permit me, I would like to take a moment to share my thoughts in my role as a very proud grandparent and great-grandparent. Beth and I have four absolutely wonderful grandchildren and five precious great-grandchildren.

Our first grandson, Mitch Tobias, Lynn and Bob's son, is a real creative talent who is starting to swing in his chosen profession. He is a photographer and he and his works have become recognized in Los Angeles, San Francisco, and New York. He married JoAnne Farrell and together they have a son Dorian, who is over a year old. Mitch's first love is music, which he continues to write and record in his spare time.

Our other two grandsons, Steve and Darren Sullivan, are Joyce's sons from a previous marriage. Steve is a great guy who is well read and who digs good classical music and good cigars. He graduated from Sound Masters Engineering School with high hopes of becoming a recording engineer. He is also an amateur photographer.

Darren is currently a college professor of theater arts and English at Ventura College. He also taught that same subject matter in New England.

Our one and only granddaughter, Allison Tobias, is a classy and beautiful young lady who was an elementary school teacher in the Los Angeles school system. It was there that she found the love of her life. She had taught three young girls who had a widowed father, Brad Bronson. After she got to know Brad through a number of Parent-Teacher Conferences, love bloomed between them. Five years ago Ali and Brad wed with a ready-made family with daughters Brittany, now age 18, McCall, now age 16, and Mia, now 11. Ali and Brad have children of their own: twins, Brooke and Andrew, who are over a year old.

Beth and I are so very happy for these four wonderful, healthy, and happy grandchildren and lovely three great-grandchildren and three step-great-grandchildren. We have wonderful relationships with all of them and we are all very close. We are truly blessed.

These blessings became even more prevalent to us when Beth and I celebrated our 70th wedding anniversary on Sunday, September 21, 2008. Our daughter Joyce opened her lovely home in Bel Air to host about 100 guests. Our children, grandchildren and great-grandchildren were there, of course, as well many of my dear friends from the music business: Butch Stone and his lovely wife Shirley; Kay Starr; Bea Wain; Lee Hale; Melissa

MacKay and her husband David, who is an outstanding jazz pianist; Ray Charles; John Clayton and his wife Tenieka; Vic Mizzy (a fine composer/ arranger who wrote the theme for television's *The Addams Family*) and his wife Shirley; and Bobbie Kahn, the widow of Donald Kahn, the son of composer Gus Kahn, among others. Award-winning columnist James Bacon also was in attendance.

In addition to delicious food, good drink, and fine company, there was also superb entertainment. A fine-sounding musical combo comprised of John Prioux (pronounced PREW), piano; Luther Hughes, string bass; and vocalists Mike and Amy Campbell filled the air with inviting sounds.

Backed by this "house band," if you will, Lee Hale and Melissa McKay got together to sing a cute original piece about the institution of marriage. Bea Wain was creative in her approach as she sang a parody about Beth and me to the tune "My Favorite Things." Ray Charles sang a jaunty parody of his own to the tune of "A-Tisket, A-Tasket," while the incomparable Kay Starr belted out a swinging rendition of "Honeysuckle Rose."

As the evening drew to a close, some of the guests, including Bea Wain, Melissa MacKay, Sue Allan, Bill Brown, and Peggy Schwartz (one of the four Clark Sisters who sang with Tommy Dorsey in the mid-1940s comprising the vocal group "The Sentimentalists" and the widow of Willie Schwartz, Glenn Miller's lead clarinetist), gathered in groups of about 5 or 6 to sing some close-knit harmony a cappella style to such standards as "Dream," "Bye, Bye Blackbird," and "A-Tisket, A-Tasket." Their fun and enthusiasm were contagious. Who said seniors can't swing?

A week before our anniversary party, Beth and I traveled to New York to spend some time alone together at the Essex House overlooking Central Park, where we were married 70 years earlier. We even slept in the same room as we had on our honeymoon night. And you know what? The same magic that Beth and I shared that first evening together as man and wife was still spellbinding seven decades later!

As Henry Youngman once said: "I've been in love with the same woman for the past 70 years. If my wife ever found out, she'd kill me!"

As I look back on my long career, I am so very grateful for the road I've traveled; for the people I've met along the way; for the small measure of success that I have had. But most of all, I am grateful for the love and respect of our beautiful family. Now I ask you in all sincerity, what more success could a man have or want?

Here I am at home in March 2008 standing next to my three Emmy nominations that adorn my office wall.

– Photo by Stephen Fratallone

Left: An early Christmas family photo of Beth, Lynn, Joyce and me after we moved to Los Angeles.

Above: A recent photo of our daughter Joyce Harris and our granddaughter Ali Bronson. Aren't they beautiful?

Above: A family photo with our daughters and their husbands: Lynn and
Bob Tobias (left), Joyce and Harv Harris (middle), and Beth and I.
This photo was taken on a cruise to the Greek Islands in 1993.

Below: Bea Wain and Melissa MacKay gather together with an unidentified guest (back
to camera) for some impromptu singing during the 70th anniversary party for Beth and
me on September 21, 2008. Taking it all in at the far right, is my daughter Joyce.

– Photo by Stephen Fratallone

Pals forever. Butch Stone and I have been dear friends for 80 years. But who's counting? Here we are pictured together at my 70th anniversary party on September 21, 2008.

– Photo by Stephen Fratallone

Below: Co-author Stephen Fratallone wanted to have this photo taken together with me at my 70th anniversary party on September 21, 2008, because he thinks I'm famous.

It's been said that behind every man there is a woman. Beth is that woman. I love her for that! As Henny Youngman used to quip: "I've been in love with the same woman for the past 70years. If my wife finds out, she'll kill me!" We are still two lovebirds at our 70th anniversary party on September21, 2008.

– Photo by Stephen Fratallone

CHAPTER TEN

GOLF STORIES

My good friend and one-time boss Gordon MacRae first introduced me to the game of golf. When I was on the road with Gordon, he would play golf almost every day and I would remain in the hotel and write arrangements or watch TV.

One day Gordon said to me, "Hey, GOMM [his nickname for me, meaning "Grand Old Man of Music"], why don't you come out to the driving range with me and see if you can hit a few balls."

I said, "Sure, why not?"

Well, to make it short, I hit a couple of good shots and I loved it. Gordon encouraged me, and was I hooked. I bought my first set of clubs. (Pings.) I took lessons and hit the driving range as often as possible and I really got better and it turned out to be a big part of my life. I discovered that most musicians and show folk played golf and it didn't matter how well you played, you could always put together a foursome of friends or colleagues and go out, try your best and have some fun and a few laughs.

In 1955, Gordon was playing at the Desert Inn in Las Vegas and down the strip at the Flamingo Billy Eckstine was appearing. They were good friends and admirers of each other's talent. So it was only natural one day for Gordon to invite Billy to a game of golf at the fabulous Desert Inn golf course.

"Meet me at the pro shop at 10 a.m.," said Gordon.

So at 10 a.m., Billy walked in with his sharp-looking outfit, and beautiful clubs and Gordon was there to greet him.

The pro said to Gordon, "Gee, Gordon, I don't know how to tell you this, but he [meaning Billy] can't play here."

Gordon said, "What are you talking about?"

The pro said, "It's in our by-laws, Gordon. He's not permitted on the course."

Billy overheard the conversation and said, "Don't worry about it, Gordon. It's their rules, so forget about it."

Gordon was furious, and actually got belligerent. He said goodbye to Billy and went right to the bar and proceeded to get a bit drunk, which led him naturally to the crap table where he promptly lost $10,000.

For the next 15 years, every time Gordon saw Billy he'd tell him, "You son of a bitch, you owe me $10,000!"

Of course, they would have a good-natured laugh over it. But it's a true story and that's the way it was in Las Vegas in those days.

I am so grateful for the day Gordon got me to go to the driving range. Imagine if I never learned to play golf, what I would have missed in life.

After playing about five years I had an established handicap of 14, which meant that I was scoring in the middle 80s. I was good enough to play with Gordon at his club, the Lakeside Country Club in Toluca Lake, California, where he played to a 2 or 3 handicap.

During one of Gordon's dates at the Fairmount Hotel in San Francisco, I met Ernie Heckscher, the hotel's bandleader for many years. We became very friendly because I conducted his band for Gordon's act.

One day he invited Gordon and me to play golf at the prestigious Olympic Club, where he was a member. Ernie was an excellent golfer, and when we met his wife Sally, Beth loved her and so we became really good friends.

Ernie wanted to record his orchestra and wanted to do it in Hollywood. He wanted me to do all the arrangements. He brought five members from his band with him and then augmented the orchestra with some of the greatest players in Hollywood. He insisted on using Manny Klein, Bobby Guy, Bill Henderson, Justin Gordon, and Irv Cottler, among others. It was the first of six albums we did together.

Ernie was independently wealthy and he insisted on using the best recording studio and hiring the best recording engineer, who was Ami Hadani. Ernie had a good reputation in San Francisco, but the albums didn't sell anywhere else. Musically, the band sounded sensational and he and I were proud of our work. We remained good friends until he died of a heart attack and passed away suddenly. He played an important part in my life. His son Earl is a talented trumpet player and singer who I talk to occasionally.

In 1969, a new country club opened in Northridge, California. It was the Porter Valley Country Club. I was on the *Dean Martin Show* at the time and there were about a dozen orchestra members, myself included, who wanted to join Porter Valley. We applied for membership together thinking perhaps we'd get a better deal. There was Herbie Harper, Tommy Tedesco, Tommy Newsom, Maurie Harris, Irv Cottler, Marty Berman, Irv Weiss, Ray Brown, and Tommy Johnson. In our group were two African Americans: Ray Brown, probably one of the greatest jazz bassist in the world, and Tommy Johnson, a marvelous bass trombonist and tuba player. However, the Porter Valley membership committee said they'd have to have a meeting about admitting them. We told the committee that if there was a problem admitting our two friends, none of us would join. The problem was immediately "solved" and we all joined. Herbie Harper, a fine trombonist who once played with Charlie Barnet and Charlie Spivak, and who later became an icon in the West Coast Jazz scene, and I remained members at PVCC until 2001.

> *"When I started out playing trombone with Midwest territory bands in the late 1930s, we couldn't afford special arrangements so we had to make do with stock arrangements that were available in music stores,"* said Herbie Harper, age 88. *"Van Alexander was our favorite writer of stock music. He managed to somehow make a nine-piece band sound like twelve. Years later I found myself in Burbank doing The Dean Martin Show playing charts written by my favorite stock arranger. Van and I became friends and played lots of golf together and became members of the Porter Valley Country Club. I feel so fortunate to have Van for a friend through 35 years of tee times. As we grew older, we made more dinner reservations than golf dates, but we could always break 100 over a meal!"*

Porter Valley Country Club was a sporty golf course. It wasn't comparable to Lakeside or Bel-Aire, but it wasn't a Mickey Mouse course either. There were occasional problems with high winds. Winds gusts could get as high as 40 miles an hour, which always ruined a game for me.

One day, Lee Trevino was a club member's guest and it was one of those real windy days. The 3rd hole is only 150 yards, but you have to hit the ball over a small lake. When the winds blow, there would be white caps on the water of that small lake and it felt like you're hitting across the North Atlantic. Ordinarily, Trevino would hit a wedge or maybe a 9-iron, but with the wind blowing the way it was, he selected a 3-iron. He got the ball up in the wind and it never reached the green.

He picked up his clubs and as he left he said, "Thanks for inviting me, but I'll never play this course again." And he never did. However, our group stayed on and had many more years of enjoyable golf—when the wind wasn't blowing.

When I arranged and conducted *The Golddiggers Chevy* series and *The Wacky World of Jonathan Winters*, I utilized a twelve-piece orchestra and everybody in the band was a golfer. One stalwart musician and wonderful guy was Harry "Sweets" Edison. We played often in a foursome with Ray Brown and Allyn Ferguson, who is a talented arranger and composer. "Sweets" would keep us in stitches with his descriptive one-liners. If I or someone would sink a twenty-foot putt, he'd say, "You're so lucky you could shit in a swingin' jug" or "Never play with anyone that would question a 10" or "Never buy a new putter until you've had a chance to throw it." He was something and when he "took a cab," the music world not only lost a superb musician, but a fine and gentle man.

My dear friend Les Brown introduced me to Bob Hope who was a good golfer all his life. I did quite a few arrangements for his nightclub acts and he invited me to play golf with him at Lakeside Country Club many times. As Bob got older he was reduced to playing just 9 holes, but he would call me personally and say, "Meet me over at Lakeside for a quick round." Of course I would never say I couldn't make it. He also had a 9-hole pitch-and-put course in his spacious land back of his home. I also played with Dolores Hope many times in Palm Springs. She was a fine golfer also.

Another friendship that I will always cherish was with Tommy Newsom, the multi-talented saxophonist and arranger who made the country love him when he was shown for many years with the Doc Severson band on *The Tonight Show*. First of all, he was a superb golfer, at one time he was a 3 or 4 handicap. He was an early member at Porter Valley but then switched over to Lakeside Country Club in Toluca Lake. Herbie Harper and I played with him often and what a dry sense of humor he had! The laughs were always there. Tommy passed away in 2006 and we miss him.

I often reflect on all the great golf courses I've played and for any golf enthusiasts reading this, I'll mention a few.

First and foremost was Pebble Beach (all four courses): Cypress Point, Spyglass, Poppy Hills and Pebble Beach.

In Los Angeles: Lakeside, Bel-Aire, Wilshire, Los Angeles Country Club, Porter Valley, Hillcrest, Brentwood, El Caballero, Mountain Gate, Griffith Park Public Courses, and Encino Public courses.

In North Carolina I played in the pro-am at Forest Oaks.

In Miami I played Doral. In Puerto Rico I played Dorado Beach. In Hawaii I played Wailai Country Club and Mauna Kaia.

In Rancho Mirage, California, I played Thunderbird, Tamerisk, Morningside, Bermuda Dunes, Indian Wells, and Mission Hills.

There must be more but I can't remember them at this time. I played golf for most of my life, and the rest of the time I just wasted.

On the green, condition on top of putter
Stroke and drop to check putter path

GOLF
DIGEST

SPECIAL TOURNAMENT ISSUE

September 1996
$4.25 CAN

20th ANNUAL
HELP YOUTH FOUNDATION
CHARITY GOLF TOURNAMENT
September 27, 1996
Braemar Country Club

I made the cover of the September 1996 issue of *Golf Digest* as Player of the Year. Too bad the publication and the award weren't real. But get a load of that backstroke!

Having some fun with golfing buddies Harry "Sweets" Edison and Herb Ellis at Porter Valley Country Club.

Left: Here I am playing a round of golf with Bob Hope at Lakeside Country Club. Bob was a wonderful golfer and he always gave me a run for my money.

CODA

When Frank Sinatra was ill, he started thinking about his mortality, so he called the pope and said, "Your Holiness, after I pass away I would like very much to be buried in the popes' courtyard."

The pope answered, "I'm very sorry, Mr. Sinatra, but that's consecrated land, just for the popes."

Frank said, "Well, I've been a good Catholic all my life and I think I should be entitled to be buried there. If it's a matter of money, just let me know."

When the pope heard money, he quickly said, "Let me have a meeting with the council and I'll get back to you."

After conferring with the council, the pope called Frank back and said, "Mr. Sinatra, the council said you could be buried here for $5,000,000."

Frank took one beat and shot back, "What! Five million dollars for just three days??"

Well, I guess it's normal for any nonagenarian to start thinking about his mortality, but in my particular situation instead of thinking about how my life is going to end, I much rather think about what a full, wonderful, and rewarding life I have had. Since I'm considered a sort of musical relic, when I'm asked to explain my longevity and good health I always say, "I never touched a cigarette, or a drink or a woman until I was 11 years old."

I have had a wonderful life, indeed. The fruits of this life have been documented in what you are holding in your hands. I am so grateful for being successful in a business I love, and for crossing paths with so many people who became lifelong friends, and for being so blessed with the love and respect of a loving family of four generations. Who could ask for anything more?

It's been said that behind every great man there's woman. Well, I would never consider myself great, but Beth has been behind me (and more often than not, right next to me) every step of the way to guide me with her love, encouragement, and wisdom. What a trooper she is!

I couldn't conclude this account of my life without including a bit of basic philosophy to which I ascribe. I once read a paragraph written by the famous author Jessamyn West and I've never forgotten it. She wrote: "Praise God, Thank God, and God, Help Me, were as natural to me as breathing. In 1920, Charles Darwin exploded the myth of Adam and Eve in the Garden of Eden. But I never suffered because of Darwin. The Red Sea, parted or not; Noah's Ark, filled or empty; Lot's wife, salt or human flesh. True or False has nothing to do with the bubble of joy I have in my breast, that I call the presence of God."

Thanks for accompanying me on this "A" Train ride from my beginnings in Harlem to where I am now in Hollywood. I hope you had an enjoyable journey. It was fun reminiscing. The final chapter of this story has by no means been written. Until such time comes, I'll keep swinging. I hope you will, too.

Van Alexander
and His Orchestra

By

Charles Garrod and Bill Korst

Published January 1991

Many thanks to George Hall, Alan Morgan,
Raymond Hair and Jerry Valaburn
For their contributions

Item Code: A. Donahue/Van

A PUBLICATION OF THE JOYCE RECORD CLUB

Box 25802, Portland, OR. 97298

Phone/fax 503 292-2281 ** regehr@comcast.net

VAN ALEXANDER AND HIS ORCHESTRA:
Dave Frankel, Sam Zakin, Hy Small(tp) Bob Negrin, Irving Sontag(tb) Sol Kane(as) Henry
Butch Stone(as/vo) Jack Greenberg, Harry Steinfeld(cl/ts/bar) Ray Barr(p) Max Cheikes(g)
George Hanrahan(b) Sid Segal(d) Shirley Brown(vo) Van Alexander(arr.)

New York, November 3, 1938

028193-1	Alexander's Swinging aVA	Bluebird 10033, Ajax JRC-5
028194-1	Where Has My Little Dog Gone? vSB	Bluebird 10030, Regal Zonophone MR2981, Ajax JRC-5
028195-1	I Found My Yellow Basket vSB&band	Bluebird 10033, Ajax JRC-5
028196-1	On the Road to Mandalay aVA	Bluebird 10073, Ajax JRC-5
028197-1	Gotta Pebble in My Shoe vBS&band	Bluebird 10030, Ajax JRC-5
028198-1	Night and Day aVA	Bluebird 10073, Ajax JRC-5, AFRS Downbeat 65

VAN ALEXANDER AND HIS ORCHESTRA:
Dave Frankel, Harry Greenwold, Milt Davidson(tp) Eddie Collier, Jerry Freuderman(tb) Sol
Kane(as) Butch Stone(as/vo) Jack Greenberg, Harry Steinfeld(cl/ts/bar) Ray Barr(p) Joel
Livingston(g/vo) George Hanrahan(b) Sid Segal(d) Jayne Dover(vo) Van Alexander(arr.)

New York, November 23, 1938

030154-1	No Star Is Lost vJD	Bluebird 10049, Ajax JRC-5, AFRS Downbeat 65
030155-1	Your Eyes Are Bigger Than Your Heart vBS	Bluebird 10063, Regal Zonophone MR2981, Ajax JRC-5
030156-1	In a Good For Nothing Mood vJD	Bluebird 10057
030157-1	I Cried For You vJD	Bluebird 10049, Ajax JRC-5
030158-1	We'll Never Know vJD	Bluebird 10057
030159-1	You're Gonna See a Lot of Me vBS	Bluebird 10063, Ajax JRC-5

Hy Small(tp) replaces Greenwold; Murray Gold(tb) replaces Collier.

New York, December 23, 1938

030764-1	The Girl Friend of the Whirling Dervish vBS	Bluebird 10092, Ajax JRC-5, AFRS Downbeat 65
030765-1	Dream Caravan vJL	Bluebird 10102, Ajax JRC-5
030766-1	F. D. R. Jones vJD	Bluebird 10092, Regal Zonophone MR3131, Ajax JRC-5, AFRS Downbeat 65
030767-1	Hey! Barber vBS&JD	Bluebird 10111, Ajax JRC-5
030768-1	Digga-Digga Do aVA	Bluebird 10102, Ajax JRC-5
030769-1	The Good Little Things You Do vJD	Bluebird 10111, Ajax JRC-5

VAN ALEXANDER AND HIS ORCHESTRA:

Dave Frankel, Hy Small, Milt Davidson(tp) Jerry Rosa, Bud Smith(tb) Sol Kane(as) Butch Stone(as/vo) Jack Shildkret, Harry Steinfeld(cl/ts/bar) Ray Barr(p) Joel Livingston (g/vo) George Hanrahan(b) Sid Segal(d) Jayne Dover(vo)

New York, January 23, 1939

031545-1	(I'm Afraid) The Masquerade Is Over vJD	Bluebird 10118, Mont Ward 7951, Ajax JRC-7
031546-1	Honolulu vBS	Bluebird 10130, Ajax JRC-7
031547-1	This Night (Will Be My Souvenir) v JD	Bluebird 10130, Ajax JRC-7
031548-1	Oh! I'm Evil vBS	Bluebird 10137, Ajax JRC-7, AFRS Downbeat 65
031549-1	Heaven Can Wait vJD	Bluebird 10118, Mont Ward 7951, Ajax JRC-7
031550-1	Honey Bunny Boo vJD	Bluebird 10137, Ajax JRC-7

Tony Antonelli(ts) replaces Shildkret; Phyllis Kenny(vo) replaces Dover.

New York, February 16, 1939

033666-1	Thursday vPK	Bluebird 10152, Ajax JRC-7
033667-1	Hooray for Spinach vBS	Bluebird 10158, Regal Zonophone MR3080, Ajax JRC-7
033668-1	Name It and It's Yours vPK	Bluebird 10152, Ajax JRC-7
033669-1	Dancing in the Dark aVA	Bluebird 10164, Ajax JRC-7
033670-1	I'm Happy About The Whole Thing vPK	Bluebird 10158, Regal Zonophone MR3080, Ajax JRC-7
033671-1	Don't Look Now vBS	Bluebird 10164, Ajax JRC-7

VAN ALEXANDER AND HIS ORCHESTRA:

New York, March 18, 1939

035305-1	Hang Your Heart On A Hickory Limb vPK	Bluebird 10181, Regal Zonophone MR3093, Ajax JRC-7
035306-1	East Side of Heaven nPK	Bluebird 10181, Regal Zonophone MR3093, Ajax JRC-24
035307-1	The Moon Of Manakoora nPK	Bluebird 10197, Ajax JRC-24
035308-1	Another Night Alone vPK	Bluebird 10197, Ajax JRC-24
035309-1	How Strange vPK	Bluebird 10189, Ajax JRC-24
035310-1	Y' Had It Commin' To You vBS	Bluebird 10189, Ajax JRC-24

Les Hines(tb) replaces Louri.

New York, April 25, 1939

036526-1	Tony's Wife	Bluebird 10271, Regal Zonohpone 24981, Ajax JRC-24, AFRS Downbeat 65
036527-1	If I Didn't Care vPK	Bluebird 10231, Ajax JRC-24
036528-1	'Way Down Yonder in New Orleans	Bluebird 10278, Ajax JRC-24, AFRS Downbeat 65
036529-1	Adios Muchachos	Bluebird 10278, Ajax JRC-24
036530-1	No Reason At All vPK	Bluebird 10231, Ajax JRC-24
036531-1	Thou Swell	Bluebird 10271, Ajax JRC-24

VAN ALEXANDER AND HIS ORCHESTRA:
Dave Frankel, Hy Small, Archie Abrams(tp) Jerry Rosa, Bill Schallenberger(tb) Sol Kane(as)
Butch Stone(as/bar/vo) Tony Antonellie, Harry Steinfeld(ts) Ray Barr(p) Joel Livingston(g/vo)
George Hanrahan(b) Harry Fulterman(d) Phyllis Kenny(vo) Van Alexander(arr.)

New York, May 25, 1939

036977-1	In the Middle of a Dream vPK	Bluebird 10297, Ajax JRC-24
036978-1	Let There Be Love vPK	Bluebird 10297, Ajax JRC-24
036979-1	Mary Lou vVA	Bluebird 10313, Ajax JRC-24
036980-1	Ay Ay Ay vBS	Bluebird 10313, Ajax JRC-24
036981-1	Begone Vpk	Bluebird 10301, Regal Zonophone MR3131, Ajax JRC-24
036982-1	You Are My Dream Vpk	Bluebird 10301, Ajax JRC-24

New York, June 21, 1939

037738-1	The Jumpin' Jive (Jim Jam Jump) vBS	Bluebird 10330, Ajax JRC-28
037739-1	LaRosita aVA	Bluebird 10338, Ajax JRC-28
037740-1	Ragtime Cowboy Joe	Bluebird 10330, Ajax JRC-28
037741-1	Stumbling	Bluebird 10338, Ajax JRC-28

VAN ALEXANDER AND HIS SWINGTIME BAND:
Walt Davidson, Bob Pearson, Hy Small(tp) Chick Dahlstein, Bill Schallenberger (Shallen)(tb/
vo) Sol Kane(as) Butch Stone(as/bar/vo) Tony Antonelli, Harry Steinfeld(ts) Ray Bar(p) Joel
Livingstone (g/vo) George Hanrahan(b) Harry Fulterman(d) Phyllis Kenny(vo) Van
Alexander(arr)

New York, August, 1939

7855	Honestly vPK	Varsity 8075, Ajax C-846
7856	In the Mood	Varsity 8065, Inco 2004, Ajax C-846
7857	Scatterbrain vPK	Varsity 8075, Ajax C-846
7858	Many Dreams Ago vPK	Varsity 8082, Ajax C-846
7859	Angry vPK	Varsity 8065, Ajax C-846
7860	Hot Dog Joe vBS	Varsity8082, Ajax C-846

New York, October, 1939

US 1070-1	Marie vBSh	Varsity 8112, Ajax C-846
US 1071-1	Yodelin' Jive vBS	Varsity 8102, Ajax JRC-28
US 1072-1	The Little Red Fox (N'ya N'ya, Ya Can't Catch Me) vPK	Varsity 8102, Inco 2004, Ajax JRC-28
US 1073-1	I Wonder Who's Kissing Her Now vBSh	Varsity 8112, Ajax C-846

New York, December, 1939

US 1148-1	I Wanna Wrap You Up (And Take You Home with Me) vPK	Varsity 8126
US 1149-1	Oh! What A Lovely Dream vPK	Varsity 8126
US 1150-1	Pinch Me vPK	Varsity 8133
US 1151-1	Prelude to the Bughouse aVA	Varsity 8133, AFRS Downbeat 65

US 1280-1	Easy Does It (Cuidadito) vPK	Varsity 8177, Ajax C-846
US 1281-1	My! My! vBS	Varsity 8172, Ajax JRC-28
US 1282-1	Say It (Over and Over Again) vPK	Varsity 8172, Ajax C-846
US 1283-1	Ho! Sa! Bonnie vBS&band	Varsity 8177, Ajax JRC-28

VAN ALEXANDER AND HIS SWINGTIME BAND
Hy Small, Bob Pearson, Walt Davidson(tp) Bill Shallen(tb/vo) Ernie Strucker(tb) Sol Kane(as) Butch Stone(as/bar/vo) John Hayes, Hank Stanley(ts) Van Alexander (p/arr) Jack Kelly(p) Joel Livingston(g/vo) Sandi Block(b) Irv Cottler(d) Phyllis Kenny(vo).

US 1518-1	Tempis Fugit aVA	Varsity 8250, Ajax JRC-28
US 1520-1	Hear My Song Violetta vPK	Varsity 8250, Ajax JRC-28

VAN ALEXANDER AND HIS ORCHESTRA
Personnel same.

US 1711-1	Cherry vBS	Varsity 8317, Ajax C-846
US 1712-1	Slap Jack vBS	Varsity 8317, Ajax C-846
US 1713-1	Six Lessons From Madame LaZonga vPK	Varsity 8312, Ajax JRC-28
US 1714-1	Please Take a Letter, Miss Brown vBSh	Varsity 8312, Ajax JRC-28

Van Alexander (vo).

US 1769-1	On Behalf of the Visiting Firemen vVA&BS	Varsity 8328, Ajax JRC-28
US 1770-1	I Can't Resist You vPK	Varsity 8335, Ajax C-846
US 1771-1	Jungle Jive vBS	Varsity 8335, Ajax C-846
US 1772-1	I Won't Go Home Till You Kiss Me vPK	Varsity 8328

Personnel unknown.

Indiana Blues	Beacon 100
Lonesome Me	-

SOUNDIES

Margie	Film Sound Track

VAN ALEXANDER AND HIS ORCHESTRA:
Buddy Colaneri, Irv Friedman, Red Schwartz, Danny Wilson(tp) Mike Cohen, Buck
Scott(tb) Frank Socolow(ts) plus 3 other saxes; Van Alexander(p/arr) Jimmy Norton(g) Louis
Spinell(b) Bobby Rickey(d) Betty Carr(vo)

July, 1943

John Austin(tp) replaced one of the above.

EWING SISTERS WITH VAN ALEXANDER TRIO

		Los Angeles, 1946
SRR 2514	Whatcha Gonna Do?	Standard Transcription R-211
	I Whistle a Happy Tune	-
	Pinones	-
	Snooky Ookums	-
	If You're Not Completely Satisfied	-
SRR 2515	Growing Pains	-
	I Really Don't Want To Know	-
	You Never Know	-
	Boogie Waiter	-
SRR 2542	The Springtime Cometh	Standard Transcription R-215
	Nebiddy Be	-
	I Love a Piano	-
	Rootin' Tootin' Cowboy	-
	C'Mon Papa	-
SRR 2543	I Won't Cry Anymore	-
	Showboat Shuffle	-
	So Long Oo-long	-
	You're So Wholesome	-
	I Don't	-
SRR 2653	Whoo-ee Loo-ee-siana	Standard Transcription R-218
	Milky Way Trolley	-
	National Week for Love	-
	If Teardrops Were Pennies	-
	Doncha Dare	-
SRR 2654	Mazeltov	-
	If I'd Only Known You Then	-
	Near To You	-
	Saw Your Eyes	-
	Grandfather Kringle	-

VAN ALEXANDER'S BLUE RHYTHM BAND:

Frank Beach, Chuck Peterson, Charlie Shavers(tp) Sid Harris, Si Zentner, Charles Maxon(tb) Eddie Rosa(cl/as) Clint Neagley(as) Stan Getz(as/ts) Lucky Thompson(ts) Butch Stone(bar) Jimmy Rowles(p) Tony Rizzi(g) Arnold Fishkin(b) Don Lamond(d) Van Alexander(arr).

		Los Angeles, May 20, 1947
ROY 176-B	Blue Rhythm Blues	Parlaphone (E) R, Ara LP100, Design DLP153, Pickwick Inter PR113
ROY 177-A	Blue Rhythm Jam	Parlaphone(E) R, Ara LP100, Design DLP153, Pickwick Inter PR113, MGM 10302
ROY 177-B	Blue Rhythm Bop	MGM 10302

JERRY WAYNE WITH VAN ALEXANDER AND HIS ORCHESTRA

		Hollywood, unknown date
30728	This Will Be a Lonesome Summer	Beacon 100
30729	Indiana Blues	Beacon 100
30730	The Watchman Fell Asleep	Beacon 101
30731	Sweetheart Serenade	Beacon 101

JERRY DUANE WITH VAN ALEXANDER AND HIS ORCHESTRA

	Hollywood, unknown date
Will You Still Be Mine?	Trend T-52
London in July	Trend T-53

KAY BROWN WITH VAN ALEXANDER AND HIS ORCHESTRA

		Hollywood, unknown date
JB306	Oop Shoop	Crown 127
JB306	Love Me	Crown 127

LEO DIAMOND WITH VAN ALEXANDER AND HIS ORCHESTRA

		Hollywood, unknown date
ARC 2001	On the Mall	Ambassador 1006
ARC 2004	Sadie Thompson's Song	Ambassador 1006

TOMMY TURNER WITH VAN ALEXANDER AND HIS ORCHESTRA

	Hollywood, unknown date
It Isn't Right	? 202
Lay Down Your Arms	? 202
(My Heart Goes) Ka-Ding Dong	? 202

VAN ALEXANDER'S BLUE RHYTHM BAND
Ray Linn, Jimmy Zito(tp) Juan Tizol(vtb) Eddie Rosa(cl/as) Willie Smith(as) Herbie
Haymer(ts) Butch Stone(bar) Moe Welscher(p) Barney Kessel(g) Arnold Fishkin(b) Irv
Cottler(d) Charles Gardle(vibes) Van Alexander(arr)

		Los Angeles, November 15, 1947
ROY 205-B	Blue Rhythm Ramble	Parlaphone(e) R, Ara LP100, Design DKP153, Pickwick Inter PR113
ROY 206-A	Blue Rhythm Bounce	Parlaphone(E) R, Ara LP100, Design DLP153, Pickwick Inter PR113

VAN ALEXANDER AND HIS ORCHESTRA

		Hollywood, 1948
48S-436	How'm I Doin'?	MGM
48S-437	Old Uncle Fud	MGM

LANCERS WITH VAN ALEXANDER AND HIS ORCHESTRA

		Hollywood, unknown period
700	So High, So Low, So Wide	London 8079
701-1	It's You, It's You I Love	London 8079

BUTCH STONE WITH VAN ALEXANDER AND HIS ORCHESTRA

		Hollywood, March, 1949
3515-1D	Etiquette Blues	Capitol 15301
	My Feet's Too Big	Capitol 15301

EWING SISTERS/JOE FINGERS CARR WITH VAN ALEXANDER AND HIS ORCHESTRA

		Hollywood, Summer, 1951
7645-2D	Ventura Boulevard Boogie	Capitol 1733
7646-2D	I Love a Piano	Capitol 1733

GORDON MACRAE WITH VAN ALEXANDER AND HIS ORCHESTRA

		Hollywood, unknown date
9105-4D	Be My Guest w/choir	Capitol 1836
9106-4D	How Close	Capitol 1846, AFRS Basic Music Library P-2228
9107	Green Acres and Purple Mountains	Capitol 1941, AFRS Basic Music Library P-2228
9108	Baby Doll	Capitol 1941, AFRS Basic Music Library P-2228
9113	My Love	Capitol 1846, AFRS Basic Music Library P-2228
	Laughing at Love	Capitol 1836

GORDON MACRAE WITH VAN ALEXANDER AND HIS ORCHESTRA

Hollywood, February, 1952

9529-3D	There's A Lull In My Life	Capitol 2196, AFRS Basic Music Library P-2507
9629	Call Her Your Sweetheart	Capitol 1990, AFRS Basic Music Library P-2228
9631-2D	Nine Hundred Miles	Capitol 1990, AFRS Basic Music Library P-2228
9879-2D	(There'll Be) Peace In The Valley (For Me)	Capitol 2114, AFRS Basic Music Library P-2507
9880-4D	Mansion Over The Hilltop	Capitol 2114, AFRS Basic Music Library P-2507
9895-6D	Blame It On My Youth	Capitol 2196, AFRS Basic Music Library P-2507
	These Things Shall Pass	AFRS Basic Music Library P-2301
	Gentle Hands	AFRS Basic Music Library P-2301
	No Other Girl	AFRS Basic Music Library P-2507
	If Someone Had Told Me	AFRS Basic Music Library P-2507

CHARLIE CAL WITH VAN ALEXANDER AND HIS ORCHESTRA

Hollywood, unknown date

50-302	Soothe My Aching Heart Tonight	Songbird 201
50-303	The Devil's Bride	Songbird 201

ART LUND WITH VAN ALEXANDER AND HIS ORCHESTRA

Hollywood, December 1950

50S-3156-4	Velvet Lips	MGM 10878
50S-3157-2	Nuthin' Like You	MGM 10878, AFRS Basic Music Library P-1879
50S-3158-3	Have a Piece of Wedding Cake	MGM 10915
50S-3159	Nice Work If You Can Get It	UNISSUED
50S-206	Somebody Stole My Horse and Wagon	MGM 10915

MOLLY BEE WITH VAN ALEXANDER AND HIS ORCHESTRA

Hollywood, November, 1952

10701-1N	I Saw Mommy Kissing Santa Claus	Capitol 2285
10702-2N	Willy Claus	Capitol 2285
11096-1D	What'll He Do?	Capitol 2396
11098-1D	Dancin' With Someone	Capitol 2396

MEL BLANC WITH VAN ALEXANDER AND HIS ORCHESTRA

Hollywood, March, 1953

11208-1N	The Little Red Monkey	Capitol 2430, AFRS Basic Music Library P-2931
	Tia Juana	Capitol 2430
11769-1D	Yah, Das Ist Ein Christmas Tree	Capitol 2619
	I Can't Wait till Quithmuth Day	Capitol 2619

CURLY WIGGINS WITH VAN ALEXANDER AND HIS ORCHESTRA

Hollywood, 1953

53S-3131	Holes in My Head	MGM 11773
53S-3132	These Things Change	MGM 11773
53S-3133	Ambushed	MGM 11679
53S-3134	Wilderness	MGM 11679

GORDON MACRAE WITH VAN ALEXANDER AND HIS ORCHESTRA

Hollywood, October 12, 1953

11960	Never in a Million Years	Capitol 2652, AFRS Basic Music Library P-3256
11979	Stranger in Paradise	Capitol 2652, AFRS Basic Music Library P-3256

MOLLY BEE WITH VAN ALEXANDER AND HIS ORCHESTRA

Hollywood, January, 1954

12290-1N	Remember Me	Capitol 2741, AFRS Basic Music Library P-3503
	Pine Tree, Pine Over Me	Capitol 2741, AFRS Basic Music Library P-3503
12291-1N	In the Pyrenees	Capitol 2790, AFRS Basic Music Library P-3503

GORDON MACRAE WITH VAN ALEXANDER AND HIS ORCHESTRA

Hollywood, January, 1954

12304	Stuffy	Capitol 2790, AFRS Basic Music Library P-3503

JUD CONLON RHYTHMAIRES WITH VAN ALEXANDER AND HIS ORCHESTRA

Hollywood, March, 1954

A Kiss in the Dark	Vito ??

ALEXANDER, PAGE 8

GORDON MACRAE WITH VAN ALEXANDER AND HIS ORCHESTRA

Hollywood, Summer, 1954

12460-1N	Coney Island Boat	Capitol 2784
	Backward, Turn Backward	AFRS Basic Music Library P-3457
	Soothe My Lonely Heart	AFRS Basic Music Library P-3457

GORDON MACRAE AND JUNE HUTTON WITH VAN ALEXANDER AND HIS ORCHESTRA

Hollywood, Summer, 1954

Open Your Arms	Capitol 2784
Tik-A-Tee Tik-A-Tay	Capitol 3085
Tell Me That You Love Me	Captiol 3085

MEL BLANC WITH VAN ALEXANDER AND HIS ORCHESTRA

		Hollywood, Summer, 1954
12607-1D	Woody Woodpecker and the Truth Tonic	Capitol 32156
	Pied Pipe Pussycat	Capitol 11754, 32127

GORDON MACRAE WITH VAN ALEXANDER AND HIS ORCHESTRA

		Hollywood, Fall, 1954
12988-2N	Cara Mia	Capitol 2927
12989-2N	Count Your Blessings (Instead of Sheep)	Capitol 2927

LANCERS WITH VAN ALEXANDER AND HIS ORCHESTRA

		Hollywood, October, 1954
WL7942-2A	Mister Sandman	Coral 61288
WL7943-1A	The Little White Light	Coral 61288
WL7979-6A	'Twas the Night Before Christmas	Coral 61314
WL7980-5A	I Wanna Do More Than Whistle	Coral 61314
WL8509-2A	The Walking Doll	Coral 61550

ANDY WILLIAMS WITH VAN ALEXANDER AND HIS ORCHESTRA

	Hollywood, unknown date
Why Should I Cry Over You?	X-0036
You Can't Buy Happiness	X-0036

Doris Day(vo).

	1953	
I Can't Give You Anything But Love vDD	Transcription, Hindsight 200	
Sentimental Journey vDD	-	-
You Oughta Be in Pictures vDD	-	-
Blue Skies vDD	-	-
Be Anything But Be Mine vDD	-	-
My Blue Heaven vDD	-	-
Love to Be With You vDD	-	-
Don't Worry 'Bout Me vDD	-	-
I'm a Big Girl Now vDD	-	-
Everything I Have Is Yours vDD	-	-
A Hundred Years From Today vDD	-	-
I've Gotta Sing Away These Blues vDD	-	-
I've Got It Bad and That Ain't Good vDD	-	-

DORIS DAY WITH VAN ALEXANDER AND HIS ORCHESTRA

		Hollywood, December, 1955
CO 55111	I've Gotta Sing Away These Blues	Columbia 40704

<u>LORRY RAINE WITH VAN ALEXANDER AND HIS ORCHESTRA</u>

<u>Hollywood, unknown date</u>

E40B4117   I'll Tell the World I Love You   Dot   15173

On October 7, 1957, Van Alexander and his Orchestra began with The Guy Mitchell Show on ABC. This weekly show continued until January 13, 1958.

VAN ALEXANDER AND HIS ORCHESTRA:
Conrad Gozzo, Manny Klein, Van Rasey, Shorty Sherock(tp) Joe Howard, Eddie Kusby, Tommy Pederson(tb) Ken Shroyer(btb) Paul Horn, Abe Most(cl/as) Plas Johnson, Jules Jacobs(ts) Butch Stone(bar) Paul Smith(p) Barney Kessel(g) Joe Comfort(b) Irv Cottler(d) Van Alexander(arr).

<u>Hollywood, 1959</u>

Let's Get Together	Capitol ST/T1243, ST/T1712, 054-81711
Chant of the Weed	- - -
East St. Louis Toodle-oo	- - -
Ride, Red, Ride	- - -

VAN ALEXANDER AND HIS ORCHESTRA:
Conrad Gozzo, Manny Klein, Shorty Sherock(tp) Milt Bernhart(tb) Ronnie Lang, Abe Most(cl/as) Plas Johnson(ts) Chuck Gentry(bar) Ray Sherman(p) Barney Kessel(g) Joe Mondragon(b) Shelly Manne(d) Van Alexander(arr).

<u>Hollywood, 1959</u>

Until the Real Thing Comes Along	Capitol ST/T1243, ST/T1712, 054-817111
Uptown Rhapsody	- - -
I Would Do Anything for You	- - -
A-Tisket A-Tasket	- - -

VAN ALEXANDER AND HIS ORCHESTRA:
Shorty Sherock, Manny Klein(tp) Milt Bernhert(tb) Ronnie Lang, Abe Most(cl/as) Plas Johnson(ts) Chuck Gentry(bar) Jeff Clarkson(p) Barney Kessel(g) Joe Mondragon(b) Shelly Manne(d) Van Alexander(arr).

<u>Hollywood, 1959</u>

Stompin' at the Savory	Capitol ST/T1243, ST/T1712, Undecided
	- -
Organ Grinder's Swing	- -
Christopher Columbus	- - , 054-81711

VAN ALEXANDER AND HIS ORCHESTRA
Personnel unknown.

	Hollywood, 1961
Melancholy Serenade	Capitol ST/T1457
I'll Be Seeing You	-
My Tani	-
Auf Wiedersehen	-
Autumn Leaves	-
Auld Lang Syne	-
The Last Dance	-
Sweetheart of Sigma Chi	-
The Last Call	-
Moonlight Sonata	-
I'll See You in My Dreams	-
Goodnight Sweetheart	-

VAN ALEXANDER AND HIS ORCHESTRA:
Joe Graves, Shorty Sherock(tp) Milt Bernhart, Dick Kenney, Lew McGreary(tb) Mahlon Clark, Eddie Rosa(cl/as) Julie Jacob, Plas Johnson, Babe Russin(ts) Henri Rose, Bob Stevenson(p) Shelly Manne, Alvin Stoller, Frank Guerrero, Irv Cottler, Milt Holland, Jack Havarra(d/perc) Van Alexander(arr).

	Hollywood, 1962	
Get Me to the Church on Time	Capitol ST/T1635,	054-81711
I Won't Dance	-	-
'Way Down Yonder in New Orleans	-	-
In a Mellow Tone	-	-
Stealin' Apples	-	-
Tappin' on the Traps	-	-
Ol' Man River	-	-
Lulu's Back in Town	-	-
High Noon	-	-
Say It Isn't So	-	-
Blues in Twos	-	-
Strike Up the Band	-	-

They say there's nothing like a good book...

We think that says quite a lot!

BearManorMedia

P O Box 71426 • Albany, GA 31708
Phone: 760-709-9696 • Fax: 814-690-1559
Book orders over $99 always receive FREE US SHIPPING!
Visit our webpage at www.bearmanormedia.com
for more great deals!

Printed in the United States
219618BV00002B/5/P